THIS CONSTANT EVIL

THE INVENTION OF ETHNIC CLEANSING

James Shepherd-Barron

RUNWAY
PUBLISHING

This Constant Evil

Published by Runway Publishing
The Pill Box, 115 Coventry Road, London E2 6GG
www.runwaypublishing.co.uk

First edition, July 2021

ISBN: 978-1-8384901-4-0

DEDICATION

For those who suffered—and still suffer—the horrors of ethnic cleansing. And for those who bear witness.

What's the cost of lies?

It's not that we'll mistake them for the truth.

The real danger is that if we hear enough lies then we no longer recognise the truth at all.

What do we do then?

What else is left but to abandon even the hope of truth and content ourselves instead with stories.

In these stories, it doesn't matter who the heroes are;

All we want to know is who to blame.

Reflections on the dangers of false narrative by Valery Legasov (played by Jared Harris in HBO's award-winning 2018 docudrama mini-series, *Chernobyl*) before committing suicide two years to the minute after the nuclear power-plant accident in Soviet Russia on 26th April 1986.

'THE SITUATION SEEMS A TEXTBOOK EXAMPLE OF ETHNIC CLEANSING.'

ZEID RA'AD AL-HUSSEIN, U.N. High Commissioner for Human Rights, accusing Myanmar authorities of intentionally driving out the more than 313,000 Rohingya Muslims who have fled to neighboring Bangladesh, in a keynote address before the U.N. Human Rights Council in Geneva

This full-page ad in the New York Times appeared on 15 November 2017. Within months, the UN no longer referred to the forced expulsion of the Rohingya from Myanmar in terms of 'ethnic cleansing', preferring instead to use the less emotive term 'crime against humanity'. Part of the rationale for this linguistic two-step was because the term 'ethnic cleansing' has no legal meaning in an international criminal court. This book explains why, and what more could be done to stop such murderous practices in future.

CONTENTS

PROLOGUE

THIS BROADCAST BY ALLAN LITTLE was made on 11th July 2020 by BBC Radio to mark the 25th anniversary of the Srebrenica massacre—the worst atrocity on European soil since the defeat of Nazi Germany—and is reproduced verbatim with the permission of the BBC[1].

> *Bosnian Serb forces besieged and bombarded the town of Srebrenica[2] for three years then seized it in July 1995. The men and older boys were separated from their families and the killing began. The enclave had been declared a UN safe zone two years earlier but nothing was done to make it safe. A small,*

---

1. BBC Radio-4, Today Programme; 11 July 2020
2. Pronounced 'Sre-bren-eetsa'

> *lightly-armed Dutch peacekeeping force couldn't stop the massacre. The Dutch also handed over to the Serbs thousands of terrified Muslims who had crowded into the UN compound seeking refuge. Srebrenica was the atrocity that finally led to the Western military intervention the Muslim-led Bosnian government had been begging for.*
>
> *The International Criminal Tribunal for the former-Yugoslavia (ICTY) at the Hague would later rule that what happened at Srebrenica constituted genocide. But it was different only in scale to atrocities that had characterised the Bosnian war from the start: Mass murder as a means to pursue an ethnically pure territory in a campaign of pure violence that gave to the lexicon of conflict a chilling new euphemism... 'ethnic cleansing'.*

In 2017, twenty-two years after the fact, the infamous Serb commander Ratko Mladić was convicted of genocide for the Srebrenica killings. The International Criminal Tribunal for the former-Yugoslavia also found him guilty on five counts of crimes against humanity and four war crimes, including the bombardment of Sarajevo and holding UN peacekeepers hostage.

By the Summer of 2020, the ICTY appeals chamber was in a race with the 77-year-old war criminal's fading health to complete the legal process of holding him to account whilst he was still alive. One year later, he lost his final appeal and will spend the rest of his life behind bars.

FOREWORD

THIS IS A STORY OF FAILURE. And of man's inhumanity to man. When I first went to Croatia in January 1992, smoke from the ruins of Vukovar still hung thin and limpid in the crisp Slavonian air. The squalid victory of ethnic nationalism and of fascism, though gathering momentum, was yet to impinge on the wider world. The Serbo-Croat war, ignited the previous Summer after the secession of Slovenia from the former-Yugoslavia, had become bogged down in the leafy outskirts of small market-towns like Osijek and Vincovci in East Slavonia. The Bosnian war, with its secret concentration camps, Sarajevo's and Srebrenica's, had not yet started. What the world would soon come to know as the 'ethnic cleansing' of non-Serb populations was spreading South and becoming more brazen.

Writing a couple of years later, this is how the war journalist David Rieff described what was going on at the time in his book *Slaughterhouse Bosnia*:

> *It is hard to be dispassionate about ethnic cleansing and mass murder and I just had to write as frankly as I could of my journeys to the slaughterhouse that the Republic of Bosnia-Herzegovina became in the Spring of 1992. Thanks to the heroic efforts of a few aid workers and journalists, stories of atrocity were already leaking out.*
>
> *It was hard to be dispassionate but if the bad news could just be brought home to people, I remember thinking, the slaughter would not be allowed to continue. When I first started going to Bosnia, my hope was to add my voice to those far braver than I who were risking their lives to bear witness to what was taking place there. We did not just think that what was going on was a tragedy—all wars are tragic—but that the values that the Republic of Bosnia-Herzegovina exemplified were worth preserving. Those ideals of a society committed to multiculturalism and tolerance, and of an understanding of national identity as deriving from shared citizenship rather than ethnic identity were precisely the ones which we in the West so assiduously proclaim. And I had not been long in Bosnia before I came to believe, as I continue to believe today, that we in the rich world had not only a moral obligation to defend Bosnian independence but a compelling interest in doing so as well. That campaign has been lost. What remains is the obligation to bear witness, the obligation to the dead as well as to the living.*

Ethnic Cleansing has been a constant evil in world history. Most of us are who we are because we are the direct descendants of those lucky enough to survive its hideous practices and vile effects. Yet while everyone seems to know intuitively what it's not, no-one seems able to define what it is.

Is it just a lazy synonym for Genocide? Or, as Allan Little, the former BBC correspondent suggests, a lesser euphemism for war crimes? Is it just another form of human rights violation? Or is it something else?

As a construct, the form of atrocity implied by the term 'ethnic cleansing' forces us to confront some ugly truths about ourselves and ask 'who is the better angel here?' What depths of hatred are required to persuade people not so different from us to take part in mass murder and to believe when doing so they are involved in something heroic, even virtuous?

How can it be that this most primaeval and dangerous of emotions has been consciously stoked and manipulated throughout history, drawing ordinary people into committing acts of extraordinary barbarity? How is it possible that mere words inspire people to such violence? How can history be weaponised to the point that tens of thousands of people are murdered for the simple crime of being 'other'?

In one of the final scenes of the final episode of the final series of the blood-soaked televisual rollercoaster that is *Game of Thrones*, an exhausted and humbled Tyrion (played magnificently by

Peter Dinklage) muses to an assembled council on what it is when all has been said and done that unites people: 'Armies?... Gold?... Flags?' he asks.

Casting a battle-scarred and world-weary gaze over an array of cousins who have just spent years trying to kill each other, he pauses for dramatic effect before providing his own answer: 'Stories,' he says. 'There is nothing in the world more powerful than a good story. Nothing can stop one. No enemy can defeat one. Stories are our memory; the keeper of our secrets; our triumphs; our defeats; our past... our history.'

He was right, of course; humans are susceptible to storytelling. Stories can be a very useful way of remembering history and of conveying interesting truths and facts. But they can just as easily be turned against us; telling us anything, but teaching us nothing.

Tyrion's soliloquy was prefaced with musings by the assembled council over the futility of war. 'We have been cutting each other's throats long enough,' one member said, before going on to reflect '... and we know how that ends.' Given that almost everyone in this award-winning show comes to a grisly end, indeed we do.

The cast could have been describing 'ethnic cleansing'. After all, this world-renowned TV series, being an allegory on the feuding between family, clan, tribe and ethnic group in the struggle for power and national self-determination, was only reflecting the popular academic thesis that institutionalised warfare, fratricide and internecine murder gave us the world we know today.

From Syria to Sudan, Burundi to Myanmar, and China to Ukraine it can even be argued this abhorrent practice is shaping it still.

Essentially, the story of ethnic cleansing is a story about the cost of lies; about filling in the gaps between myth and reality, the present and the past. And when people choose to lie, when other people choose to believe the lie, and when everybody engages in a passive conspiracy theory to promote the lie over the truth, whole societies become capable of suspending disbelief. The people who ultimately suffer are not the people who tell the lie... it's those that believe them.

The term 'ethnic cleansing' only came to the public's attention in the Spring of 1992. It has been gaining universal recognition ever since.

Yet, despite the constant references in the media and elsewhere, few people understand what it means or know from where it was derived. As the lawyer Drazen Petrovic explained when attempting to outline the methodology behind it in 1994[3], 'The reasoning behind the terminology and its relationship to the system of international law are not very clear.'

---

3. Petrovic: Ethnic Cleansing—An Attempt at Methodology; European Journal of International Law, Vol.5, 1994

Even today, over twenty-five years later, the United Nations' Office on Genocide Prevention[4] cannot provide a definition, its website stating that 'The term surfaced in the context of the 1990's conflict in the former Yugoslavia. However, the precise roots of the term or who started using it and why are still uncertain.'[5]

Such lack of definition has hindered legal attempts to prosecute and hold war criminals to account, and obscures wider public understanding of the political underpinnings of this obscenity.

Thus far in the history of international humanitarian and human rights law, the term has been applied more for emotional and political reasons than legal. That the international community has employed the term as an excuse not to comply with duties laid down by their obligations under the Genocide Convention as some observers suggest can no longer be a valid reason for not providing such a definition.

It is precisely because the phrase does not exist in international humanitarian and human rights law that it continues to cause more confusion than clarification.

Take the case of Myanmar, where the country's military have been systematically killing members of the Rohingya ethnic minority since late 2017. As in Rwanda, Sudan, Syria and else-

---

4. The United Nations 'Office on Genocide Prevention and the Responsibility to Protect' is an office within the UN's Department of Political Affairs in New York.
5. https://www.un.org/en/genocideprevention/ethnic-cleansing.shtml (accessed 24 June 2021)

where, a shocked world expressed its moral outrage, with the UN's top human rights official at the time describing what was going on as 'a classic example of ethnic cleansing'. The US House of Representatives followed suit a few months later, passing a resolution condemning 'the ethnic cleansing of the Rohingya.'

Yet, two years later, in October 2019, when fifty-seven nations filed suit at the International Court of Justice, alleging that the government of Myanmar was responsible for 'creating conditions which are genocidal in character because they are intended to destroy the Rohingya group in whole or in part' no mention was made of 'ethnic cleansing'.

Some lawyers argue that it doesn't need to, as acts that might constitute 'ethnic cleansing' are captured under existing laws on 'genocide' and 'crimes against humanity'.

But the government of Myanmar was notably not being accused of genocide, only of 'creating conditions which are genocidal in character,' an altogether less substantial charge. Which is the lesser evil here? As with proceedings in the International Criminal Tribunal for the former-Yugoslavia (ICTY)[6] a decade earlier, such obfuscation makes it more likely, not less, that those responsible get away with mass murder.

---

6. Until it was dissolved in 2017, the International Criminal Tribunal for the former-Yugoslavia (ICTY) was a United Nations court of law that dealt with war crimes that took place during the conflicts in the Balkans in the 1990's. It was the first tribunal of its kind since Nuremberg at the end of the Second World War.

After sitting for 10,800 days, hearing 4,650 witnesses and digesting 2.5 million pages of transcripts, ICTY delivered a total of 161 indictments against war criminals from all over former-Yugoslavia, including against the infamous 'Butchers of Bosnia'—former Serbian president Slobodan Milošević, the Bosnian Serb leader Radovan Karadžić, and General Ratko Mladić—each of whom was accused of crimes against humanity.

Surprisingly, none of these indictments made any direct reference to the 'ethnic cleansing' strategy driving the most grisly and high-profile of their collective atrocities. Partly, this was because there was—and still is—no precise legal definition of what it entails. As a result, and despite it being used euphemistically in UN Security Council Resolutions and ICTY judgments over the years since 1992, 'ethnic cleansing' has never been recognised as an independent crime under international humanitarian or human rights law.

Whether genocidal in intent or not, 'ethnic cleansing' in Myanmar is clearly the de facto reality on the ground, with hundreds of thousands killed, disappeared or forced into squalid settlements across the border in Bangladesh.

Despite many of its practices falling within the scope of the Genocide Convention[7], it is time 'ethnic cleansing' be formally adopted as a war crime in its own right. For this to happen, the

7. In February 2015, the International Court of Justice ruled that atrocities committed in Vukovar and elsewhere in Croatia did not constitute genocide.

genesis of the term must be clarified once and for all, and a definition of the term provided. It is, after all, only by providing such definition that we can make sense of a rules-based world in which politicians and perpetrators can be fully brought to account[8].

There is precedent for this. Like the word 'genocide'—a term defined by the legal profession only in 1948 for the Nuremberg war crimes trials following the end of the Second World War—the term 'ethnic cleansing' is an invention; an artificial construct describing—and at the same time, masking—the complex and brutal reality it so blandly describes. And, as with 'genocide', it has its own story[9].

This is that story. It is told here for the first time because the truth doesn't care; it gets us all in the end. Holding people to account is where the truth is. As eminent human rights lawyer Philippe Sands put it in his book *East-West Road*, 'The real value of truth over story is only to be found in the courtroom.'

---

8. In this sense, it is essential that any new definition not be used to replace already existing definitions in international law.
9. The story of 'genocide' is told by Philippe Sands in his book *East West Road*

MINEFIELD

ONE OF MY EARLIEST boyhood memories is of my grandfather, a smiley, pipe-smoking Scotsman called Kenneth Murray, eating his porridge every morning standing up looking out of the window. At the time, I thought this was just the dotty behaviour of a grey-haired old man with a keen sense of humour and a bad back. But years later, in a more serious moment, he told me that eating one's porridge standing up was an important ritual for him; an ancient Highland tradition connected to the mass murder over two hundred years earlier of thirty-seven members of the MacDonald clan by their guests, the Campbells, in a national disgrace we now know as 'The Glencoe Massacre'.

My recollection of this story is not a matter of ethnic chauvinism but to point out that being

Scottish turns out to be more than just a matter of nationality, or place of origin, or clan, religion, or even culture. It's a state of mind, a way of viewing the world and our place in it. Looking out for the Campbells while eating your porridge is so deeply rooted in folklore and myth in the Scottish Highlands that I had grown up missing its significance, not to mention the story behind it.

From my vantage point at the top of the cliffs behind the gently decaying house, I could peer past Inverness in the distance down the length of the Great Glen and, with a bit of imagination, glimpse the summit of Ben Nevis guarding the entrance to Glencoe. Across the Firth to the South, clearly visible in the late-summer sun, lay the battlefield of Culloden where Highland clans made their final futile attempt to take on the English in 1745. And to the North, as far as the eye could see lay the heather-clad mountains of Sutherland, witness to the Highland Clearances which began fifty years later. In a sense, I was brought up surrounded by the full tragedy of the Scottish Highlands where, for time immemorial, Celt had been pitted against Viking, Pict against Scot, Highlander against Lowlander, Catholic against Presbyterian, and, most tragic of all, Clan against Clan. In some ways the story of 'cleansing', ethnic or otherwise, was in my blood.

Of all the historical tragedies to befall the Scottish Highlands, the Clearances—the terrible eviction of tens of thousands of Highland crofters from their ancestral lands by their landlords—must be the saddest. There is a misconception that the

English were really to blame and that there must somehow have been an ethnic dimension to all this. Certainly this is how the locals see it, even now. But, while there might be an element of truth in all this, it was just as much about the economics of progress. As Arthur Herman put it in his book *The Scottish Enlightenment*, 'Adam Smith's division of labour had finally arrived in the Highlands. When it did, it swept aside everything in its path. It spelled the end of the traditional Highland village community, with its complex and unspoken web of rights, powers and obligations sheltering in the Glen. When the Clan Chief began to think in terms of profit and improvement, rather than rewarding generations of loyalty and service, the old way of life, fragile even in the best of times, was doomed.' Nor were the Clearances the result of the defeat at Culloden. Almost 50 years had lapsed before the first forced clearings of villages and farms got underway to open up the land for grazing. Landlords were responding to economic rather than political pressures.

That the idea persists is down in large part to the romanticism of the great Scottish writer, Sir Walter Scott, whose stories had a way of making the past come alive through an intriguing blend of imaginative fantasy and fidelity to historical truth. Scott not only invented the modern historical novel, but one of its enduring themes: the idea of cultural conflict. He revealed to his readers that the development of civilisation does not leave clean or neat breaks; one stage does not effortlessly pass on to the next. They overlap and clash, and individuals get caught in the gap. His heroes find themselves culturally at odds with their world, and even with their own identities. And which side is superior, and which deserves to lose, is never fully resolved. The lesson was clear and simple: the past does not have to die; it can help live on in a nation's memory to determine the future.

'Scotland is indefinable,' wrote Robert Louis Stevenson, 'it has no unity except upon the map.' By the time I arrived in the Balkans, I discovered that this was true of all nations and nationalities. Scotland, Great Britain, and the United Kingdom are all artificial inventions, social constructs forged by history and tempered by time. This means that nations are human things, made for human ends and human needs. This makes them all the more interesting and valuable. But also more dangerous.

In the case of Scotland, gripped as it is by resurgent nationalism, the process of reinvention is revisionist and looks to the future through the cracked rear-view mirror of its past: Picts and Celts; the declaration of Arbroath; and the twin heroes of the Scottish Wars of Independence, William Wallace and Robert the Bruce. Scotland's ancient folk traditions and its unique culture are glorified. Whisky, haggis and the bagpipes are not there just to raise tourist revenue; like it's educational, legal, and banking systems, all of which are unique too, no opportunity is missed to show how different Scotland is to England.

And it was becoming abundantly clear to me that this was as true for a post-modern Serb factory-worker and Croat postman as it was for a Scottish crofter and English soldier.

Arriving in Zagreb, Croatia's capital in January 1992 and leaving after the fall of Knin in the Summer of 1995, I watched the Bosnian war unfold from end to ugly end. As a humanitarian adviser in the European Community Monitor Mission (ECMM)[10], I witnessed the barbarity of what was going on around me and coined the term 'ethnic cleansing' to describe it.

I don't pretend that my story is anything more than a footnote to history, particularly the history of Yugoslavia which imploded in tragic fashion under the weight of its own religious, ethnic, and cultural tensions following the dismantling of communism in Soviet Russia after 1989.

Inevitably, though, a fuller understanding of what was going on at the time requires some contextual knowledge of the place, it's geography, and its history. But this is the Balkans. And very few people, then as now, pretend they understand the Balkans.

The geographic area over which the story roams is known as 'The Krajina'[11], a zone rather than a line on a map, which in Serbo-Croat means 'Frontier' or 'Edge'.

---

10. The European Community Monitor Mission to the former Yugoslavia was established to monitor a series of ceasefire agreements in 1991 and ran until 2007.
11. Krajina is pronounced 'Cry-ee-na'

For centuries it was the badlands, marking the frontier between two great Empires, the Austro-Hungarian and the Ottoman. It was—as Croats will always remind you if they get half a chance—the border between East and West; between Christianity and Islam; by extension, between order and chaos; and, ultimately, between good and evil.

As ever in the Balkans, this sort of rhetorical and emotive description of history is somewhat more complicated and nuanced than that. But, for now, all we have to know is that centuries of wrestling over land had resulted in a patchwork of different ethnic groups living as minorities on the 'wrong' side of this ill-defined border which snakes for 875 kilometres from the Danube in the North-East to the Montenegrin coast in the South-West.

After World War II was over, it seemed that the demon of ethnic enmity had been excised from Yugoslavia. All major indigenous nationalities were given relatively wide autonomy within the federal structure, and even non-Slav Albanians and Hungarians enjoyed limited local autonomy. That Yugoslavia experienced no major outbreaks of interethnic violence was credited to Tito. However, by May 1980, with Tito gone, it became increasingly clear that the country could not be held together. The mass exodus of non-Muslim, mostly Serbian, population from Kosovo in 1981 gave Serb politicians every opportunity to pander to a long-held Serbian yearning for a strong Serbia that would unite and protect all Serbs, wherever they were. The events in Kosovo caused Serbs to reconsider and reject the relatively conciliatory 1974 constitution, which was the foundation of Yugoslav unity. Whatever the price they would have to pay, they would not relinquish their hegemony without a fight.

For their part, the Croats, and, to an extent, the Slovenes, felt that their wealth and resources were being disproportionately syphoned off and squandered in a mismanaged attempt by Belgrade to help Serbia and the less-developed republics of Montenegro, Macedonia, and Bosnia. They decided that they would be better off on their own.

As a first step, Croatia and Slovenia proposed in October 1990 a looser federation—a confederation, in effect—which the Serbs would not accept since they perceived it as the first step towards the dissolution of Serbia. The walkout of the Slovenian delegation from the 14th extraordinary Congress of the league of Communists of Yugoslavia on 22 January 1990 marked the beginning of the end of the Federation.

On 25 June 1991, Croatia and Slovenia declared their independence. Within days, fighting erupted in Serbian-inhabited parts of Krajina, which comprised 15% of the territory and 12% of the population of Croatia. The war was on.

In October 1991, Muslim and Croat representatives voted for Bosnia's sovereignty and a popular referendum was held on 29th February and 1st March 1992 which, again boycotted by the Serb minority, showed a strong preference on the part of the Muslims and Croats for an independent Bosnia.

When things began to fall apart for Yugoslavia in 1991 and fighting began to escalate, a peace plan was negotiated by former US Secretary of State Cyrus Vance to halt the fighting. Unfortunately, by the time it had been ratified, those Serbs living in that part of Bosnia now calling itself the Republic of Serbian Krajina had effectively already annexed large parts of territory which the Croats deemed to be in Croatia.

The UN was tasked to protect these contested areas while a political settlement could be found. As is usual in such things, the UN protection force (UNPROFOR) did not start to arrive until 8 March, some three months later. By then the damage was done. Ground which had previously been held by old men with shotguns was now protected by fit young men with automatic weapons in front-line trenches. Minefields sprouted between un-harvested fields of rotting maize, and the entire length of the Krajina became the largest and longest strip of no-man's-land seen in Europe since the First World War.

And one frosty Spring morning, I stepped into it.

EAST SLAVONIA

STEPPING OUT FROM the shadows, I walked slowly forward.

'Keep close,' I hissed over my shoulder.

Dünya, my interpreter, followed, pressing so close behind me I could feel the buckles of her body armour through my thin white jacket. I was her only protection. You bet she was close. The Croat Colonel hesitated. I didn't blame him. But then he stepped out too.

'No going back now,' I thought.

Behind me, to left and right, unseen eyes squinted nervously through telescopic sights, fingers on triggers, ready for what might happen next. Two hundred metres away, other eyes, equally narrowed, equally nervous, were doing the same. But their rifles were pointed at me.

'I can see you,' said the radio in my outstretched

hand. 'Moving now.'

Well, at least my opposite number was on his way.

'Ah yes.' I brought the radio slowly and deliberately to my mouth, 'I see you too.'

Like in the States'. Hands where they can see 'em. And no sudden movements.

My counterpart on the Serb side of the front line, all dressed in white like me, was clearly visible emerging from behind the remains of a farm building not 200 metres away. Behind him stepped two men, both in the uniform of the Yugoslav National Army, the JNA.

So far, so good.

With rubble crunching under booted feet, my senses extra-alert to any sign of trouble—anything out of the ordinary—I approached the first row of mines. This was expected. This was even ordinary. At least, for them. It was far from ordinary for me. A few months ago, 'ordinary' was boarding the 07:25 commuter train from Wandsworth Common, rushing around my advertising agency all day, shmoozing with a few clients, and getting home in time to tell a 'Black Jock' bedtime story to my young son. That was ordinary.

This was so far from ordinary I might as well have been in the trenches at the Somme. The feeling of dislocation was absolute; I could have been a cameraman filming a First World War battle scene, so near but yet so disconnected from what was unfolding around me.

The mines lay, deadly and dormant, in wide green lines across the frosted tarmac, neatly spaced like pieces on a chequerboard, each with a single stalk pointing indifferently into the early morning sky. One touch, one mistake, and we would be gone, obliterated in a hail of anti-tank explosive. I'm not sure which I feared the most, the mines or the snipers.

It was eerily quiet.

The dawn chorus in these parts usually consisted of the single crack of a rifle from one side, quickly followed by a brief burst of automatic fire from the other. More for show that murderous intent. Just exhausted frightened teenagers showing they were awake.

In front of me stretched the sort of blasted wasteland my grandfather would have recognised from his World War One trench, but which I, despite having once been a soldier, never really expected to see.

Wisps of smoke hung faltering in the still dawn air, rising from craters created overnight by the intermittent mortar rounds I had been listening to all night. Animal body-parts lay strewn about, rotting in slime-filled holes created by previous barrages. To my left, obscuring the dim outline of Vukovar's crumpled water tower on the horizon, an upturned tank turret lay like a discarded frying pan, its barrel pointing accusingly at the low watery sun.

Draped over the mounds of frozen, snow-encrusted earth and casual wreckage, glinting with wintery dew, lay what looked like a giant spider's web. At first, I couldn't work out what it was. A tangle of gossamer wire?

Then it clicked. 'My grandfather wouldn't have recognised that,' I thought. Anti-tank missiles, and the wire that guides them didn't exist in his day. Everything had changed. But nothing had changed. This was Europe. It was 1992. But it might as well have been 1915. In walking into the future, I had stepped back into the past.

The three of us made it safely through the mines and continued, one behind the other, into the middle of No-Man's land. I could now see the others coming out in single file to meet us. Three men, as agreed; two in uniform, one, like me, in white. 'Why is their interpreter in uniform?' I thought to myself. 'Not only that, but a crisp, clean uniform?'

Nearly there. A few more steps to go.

Dünya was holding tight onto my arm. She was shivering. From the cold or the nerves, I couldn't tell. I didn't care about the Colonel.

Brave did not describe Dünya. What on earth was she doing here? One false move, and she'd be dead. Shot in the head by a Serb sniper with no more feeling than if he were shooting a rabbit. She knew that. Me? I was just doing my job, impartially monitoring what was meant to be a ceasefire but was in fact a war; walking through a war-zone trying to make peace, trying to avert needless death and destruction. But Dünya, all five foot five inches of her, was a petite Croat woman with blond wavy hair, a primary school teacher. What on earth had made her volunteer for this? I knew the answer, of course. Her new country. A few days ago she had been warm and safe, drawing and singing with her tiny charges. Yet here she was now, cold and frightened, facing her nemesis, ready to do her bit for the motherland by interpreting what this murderous ogre, the Serb colonel now standing before us, was about to say.

There was no protocol for this. How do you introduce two Colonels from opposing armies when, just hours earlier, their troops had been trying to kill each other? We were standing, stranded and hideously exposed in the middle of No-Man's land. If either side wanted to break this locally-arranged ceasefire, all they had to do was loose off one shot. Neither side could miss. I felt like I had walked naked onto the stage at the National Theatre in front of The Queen without knowing my lines.

My ECMM colleague, a serving Greek Air Force Officer, who had led the 'opposing team' out into this field of battle leaned forward. Without saying a word, we shook hands and stepped back, both being careful to stay on the tarmac where no mines could have been laid. This was not our war. Our job this morning was to bring the two warring parties together to discuss lasting cease-fire terms and, if the inclination was there, make arrangements for the remains of a long-dead Serb soldier to be recovered from the burned out hulk of the tank I had just passed.

In the event, we didn't have to do anything.

The two Colonels eyed each other suspiciously for a moment. They could not have been more different. The Serb, tall and immaculate with epaulettes denoting his rank, a polished JNA belt buckle and clean boots; the Croat short, overweight, and wearing a crumpled camouflage uniform—the bottom half of which did not match the top—streaked with mud, with no insignia of any kind, rope for a belt, and green wellington boots on his feet.

Dünya glanced nervously at me. I glanced nervously at the Greek. The Serb interpreter, equally well turned out, glanced nervously at Dünya.

Having still said nothing, the Colonels made the first move by saluting each other. To my surprise, the Croat's was as crisp as the former JNA officer's. 'Ah-ha; he did have some military training after all.' To my even greater surprise, the two men then embraced each other like long-lost cousins. Which should have come as no surprise, as it turns out they were.

This is the strange thing about civil war. Family members end up fighting other family members. Neighbours turn against neighbours. And workmates try their best to kill their former colleagues. It all depends on who your mother and father were.

To a foreigner unused to Yugoslav customs, casual conversation in Croatia always seemed to be on the verge of becoming a shouting match. This had always puzzled me, as how can a language containing silky phrases such as 'Dobra Večer'[12] and 'Drago mi je'[13] not be romantic? Perhaps, like

12. pronounced 'dobra-vecha' meaning 'good evening'
13. pronounced 'drago-me-yer'', meaning 'good to see you?'

'trg'[14], it was all those consonants? Or it was every other word ending in '-itch'? Or maybe they were just naturally aggressive?

'To belong is to understand the tacit codes of the people you live with; it is to know that you will be understood without having to explain yourself. People, literally and figuratively, speak your language. This is why the protection and defence of a nation's language is such a deeply emotional nationalist cause, for it is language, more than land and history, that provides the essential form of belonging... which is to be implicitly understood.' This makes it even more bizarre when listening to Serb and Croat Colonels harangue each other, because they're doing so in the same language.

So, if it wasn't resources, religion or language they were fighting over, what was left? Well, there is only one thing left, and that is ethnicity, particularly Slavic ethnicity.

According to my foreign office briefing, Slavs are the largest ethno-linguistic group in Europe. Present-day Slavic people are classified into East Slavs (chiefly Russians, Ukrainians and Belarusians), West Slavs (chiefly Poles, Czechs and Slovaks), and South Slavs (chiefly Serbs, Croats, Bosnians, Bulgarians, Slovenians, Macedonians, and Montenegrins). Slavs can sometimes be further divided along religious lines, with Orthodox Christians making up the bulk. The majority are

14. pronounced 'trrrg', meaning 'square'

defined by their use of Orthodox Eastern customs and the use of Cyrillic script, as well as their cultural influence and historical connection to the Byzantine empire. Much as they liked to tell me how non-Slavic they were, Croats are Catholic Slavs defined by their Latinate influence and heritage and geographic connection to Western Europe.

Either way, they were off, talking like ten men in the bar at half-time, with only a few minutes to say everything that needed to be said between hurried pints. Dünya could only just keep up, whispering into my ear a truncated version of what they were discussing. At first, it was along the lines of 'How's Aunt Viŝnja[15]?' and 'Did old Willi get out of Dubrovnik in time?'. It didn't take long, though, for things to degenerate. Proceedings were certainly getting louder. Dünya tried to leave out the growing number of expletives, but phrases such as, 'Why did your undisciplined rabble fire first last night, you incompetent idiot?' and 'Would you fucking stop shelling my town all night!' were being bounced back and forth with growing vigour.

'Well, at least they haven't punched other,' I thought to myself, with a wry grin. 'Or drawn pistols'… which, silly me, they couldn't because it was our job to make sure they were unarmed.

It was at this precise moment that I had my first glimpse of what extreme nationalism

15. pronounced 'Vishnia'

looked like: fat-bellied bullies, drunk on slivovica and their own brand of ethnic paranoia, trading insults with former friends and colleagues in the middle of last night's killing field. The fact that I was standing next to them, the international community personified, did not make me feel any less anxious. There I was, dressed in white like a Christmas sale tailor's dummy in a shop window on New York's Fifth Avenue, protected only by a small blue and gold armband and a ridiculous blue baseball cap. Naked does not describe the feeling. I was exposed, terribly exposed. And not just to the biting wind, but to the snipers on both sides that I knew had me in their sights.

This meeting, arranged by me to see if it was possible to get the Croats on one side and Serbs on the other to stop shooting at each other by day and bombarding each other with mortar-fire and artillery by night, was not going anywhere. The shouting match was intensifying.

I looked at my watch. Our 30 minute cease-fire, so carefully arranged over the radio with my Greek counterpart the evening before, was coming to an end.

Someone coughed softly in the distance. We were no more than 100 metres away from either of the frontlines, so hearing someone cough would have been quite possible. But, clicking into action, my brain told me this was no ordinary cough. Just as I was about to yell at everybody to get down, an explosion ripped through the ground no more than 20 metres to my left, peppering us all with clods of semi-frozen earth. My first thought was that Dünya had wandered off and stepped on an anti-personnel mine; the explosion had been far too small to be an anti-tank mine.

Looking round, all I could see was a wisp of smoke spiralling out of a small, bucket-sized crater. And Dünya. was still standing next to me. 'Of course, a mortar.' My ECMM colleague, whose reactions, I have to say, were more professional than mine, eased himself out of the frozen mud and grass, and stood up. I looked at the two Colonels. They had stopped shouting at each other, and, looking at me, were now quietly laughing.

'Izvinite (Sorry), that was my lot telling me it's time to go,' said the Serb. 'Tomorrow, same time?' responded the Croat. 'Da. Same time tomorrow.'

With that, the Serb withdrew a green metal water canteen from his brown leather satchel — all former-JNA officers carried such satchels —, took a swig, and offered it to the Croat. Taking a long pull himself, he then passed it to me. In a misplaced sense of solidarity, I put it to my mouth and swallowed. Neat šljivovića[16]. Probably 100% proof. Expecting water, I gasped involuntarily. Being a Scot, I was no stranger to whisky, but this homebrew was potent stuff.

Laughing even louder, the two Colonels took one pace back each, saluted, and turned to walk the hundred metres or so back to their lines. and I followed, with me taking up the rear. Despite the recent camaraderie, it was a long walk. The skin

---

16. Home-distilled plum brandy. Pronounced 'shli-vo-vitza'

prickled between my shoulder blades. I could feel the rifle barrels now trained on my back.

Not for the first time that day, I thought 'what the fuckity fuck am I doing here?'

This was a good question, and one I was to ask myself again many times over the next few days.

When the Berlin wall came down in 1989, my wife Tessa and I watched it live on TV from our cosy upstairs bedroom in the house we had renovated together in London. I remember even talking about the new world order this heralded, and how the three of us—our one-year-old son Rory included—should fly to Berlin to be part of it. As crowds cheered the collapse of communism across Europe, we thought, like most people, that we were about to witness a new era of liberal democracy, and that he, as its inheritor, should be there from the very beginning. We very nearly went, and I regret now not having done so.

The fact that I was here, in this churned up frozen wasteland, less than a year later cowering in cellars by night and drinking rakija in smoke-filled rooms negotiating ceasefire resolutions with bigots who gave every appearance of being nothing more than warlords, made it very clear how wrong we were. All around me, the key narrative of the new post-communist world order was nationalism, the violent disintegration of nation states, and the slow terrible slide into civil war.

Fumbling for my first cigarette of the day, I cast my mind back to my time as a peacekeeper in Beirut ten years earlier. I had been a soldier once, so should be used to such carnage. But I wasn't. Nothing prepares you for this, and, not for the first time, I thought, 'what the fuck am I doing here?!?!!?' I had come to monitor a peace, a ceasefire, but had instead somehow landed in this frozen, blasted, fucked-up place, a sitting duck in someone else's no-man's land, someone else's war. And my cheap post-communist Croat cigarette lighter wasn't working. Damn.

PEACEKEEPER TO HUMANITARIAN

SIR CHARLES LEANED forward in his green leather chesterfield to pour the tea. Behind him, through the rain-streaked window, I glimpsed a squad of guardsmen wheeling about Horseguards Parade, the muffled commands of their hapless Lieutenant just making it across Whitehall into this gloomy office. He creaked. The chair creaked. Everything creaked. After generations of empire, it had to. This was Her Majesty's Foreign and Commonwealth Office in all its carpet-worn, gilded, and over-polished glory. I had, somewhat to my surprise, been summoned for an interview.

'So, you know what an NGO is?' I wasn't sure if this was a question or a statement, so I continued to stir my tea, waiting for more.

All I knew was that the British Ambassador in Bucharest, the father of a girl I had rather fancied while at University, had asked me a few weeks earlier if I would be interested in working in Yugoslavia. I had gone to tap him up for some funding for the Romanian orphanage in which I was working as a volunteer. After a few minutes of fairly ill-informed chit-chat on my part about the state of the country, he went over to an enormous green and gold safe which had been lurking unseen in the corner behind the sofa, and, after some extended knob-twiddling, obligingly coughed up the ten million zlotties I had asked for... in cash. He had posed the question in what appeared to be more or less as an afterthought whilst showing me to the door.

'There's about to be some trouble there, you see,' he went on, pausing with his hand on the chipped glass doorknob, 'and you would seem to have the credentials that might suit us.'

So grateful was I to have secured the few pounds we needed to finish off repairing the orphanage's decrepit central heating system, that I said, 'Yes. Of course. Delighted to be of service.' Some kind of banal grovelling nonsense like that.

Which is why I been somewhat surprised, having carried out the repairs and driven our donated 8-tonne lorry back across the Carpathians to the UK, to be woken by my mother-in-law, saying that someone called Sir Charles Grey was on the line from the Foreign & Commonwealth Office.

'Our man in Bucharest tells me we should meet. Can you come up to town for a chat?' I dimly wondered how he knew who I was, far less how he got hold of me at my mother-in-law's?

Up to town? Nobody uses language like that anymore, do they? I had only been back a day. '4:30 then. Today. For tea. Goodbye.' The line went dead before I had even answered.

'Well, Sir, if ...'

'No need to call me "Sir",' interrupted Sir Charles. 'Just call me "Sir Charles".'

I swear the oil painting on the wall, a Hussar officer in all his Waterloo finery, winked at me. This is what the Foreign Office is all about, of course, to intimidate through the projection of soft power. Velvet gloves, iron fists and all that. All very well when you have a few Dreadnoughts at your disposal. I smiled inwardly to myself as I remembered my lectures from far-off Sandhurst days. Projecting power abroad is one thing, bullying some hapless, unemployed, yoghurt-knitting aid worker was quite another. But I didn't really care, this was a 'chat', not an interview, and I was a little zoned out after so many weeks working in a Romanian orphanage.

'Well, Sir Charles, if by that you mean do I know about the humanitarian imperative and ...'

'No, no, no,' Sir Charles interrupted again, 'I just mean, do you know what the letters N, G, and O stand for?'

'Non-Governmental Organisation?' I ventured lamely, somewhat thrown by the simplicity of the question.

'Excellent. Now tell me about your Army days.' After a few minutes rabbiting on about counter-insurgency operations in Northern Ireland, flying helicopters and peacekeeping in Beirut,

Sir Charles interrupted again.

'What do you feel when you see a dead body?' Years later, I found out he asked all potential recruits this slightly unnerving question. Except it wasn't unnerving to me; I had seen plenty of dead bodies before, or, more specifically, parts of dead bodies.

'Good. So the job is yours. Can you get out to Zagreb by Tuesday?'

As I was in need of a job, I didn't think it wise to ask, 'What job? Where?' So it was that a few blurry minutes later, I found myself alone on the umbrella'd blustery pavement of King Charles Street with a cheery 'We'll be in touch about the details!' ringing in my ears.

PRIDE & PREJUDICE

THAT EVENING, AS I sat writing my daily SitRep (situation report) on the press-up bench in the basement gym that served as my bed and desk, I had a chance to reflect a bit further on the extraordinary human dynamics going on around me. The genial guy who had followed me into 'no-man's land' that bitter and frosty morning, and who had ended up in a shouting match with his Serb counterpart, was fully prepared to kill a man who, only a few months before, was not only his compatriot, but his workmate. Even worse, his cousin.

I had come face-to-face with the ugly reality of nationalist fanaticism in a way that I had never witnessed as a soldier-cum-peacekeeper in Northern Ireland, Cyprus, or Lebanon. 'What on earth had driven them to such extremes,'

I thought to myself, 'and in such a short space of time?' I mean, just a few months earlier, they had been sharing meals together in the tank production facility in the Croatian border town of Slavonski Brod. Even more weird was that this factory was still working, making turrets for the new M-84 variant of the much feared Russian T-72 and 'exporting' them across the front line to be assembled, together with a chasis made in Banja Luka in Bosnia, in a Serb factory outside Belgrade for onward export to Sadaam Hussein in Iraq and Col. Ghadaffi in Libya. Go figure.

Patriotism is one thing; nationalism quite another. Patriotism, I had always thought, is about tolerance and reason. It is a love of country, of place, of culture. Nationalism, on the other hand, is a hatred of everybody else's. At least, General de Gaulle's infamous epithet was one of the lessons I had absorbed while an officer cadet at Sandhurst.

Like religion, nationalism is capable of bringing out the best in people as well as the worst. That much was already clear. It can inspire them to live and work together in pursuit of a common goal, even the common good. But here it was filling everyone I met with a terrifying, righteous certainty which seemed to be spiralling into ever-more contempt for 'other'. I had come across bigotry on a daily basis as a soldier in Northern Ireland during the early 1980's with Catholics spitting on Protestants—and vice versa—at any opportunity. I had had to deal with what happens once spitting turns to shooting and bombing. And it's not pretty. It wasn't pretty here either. Far from it.

So, here I was, cold and tired being forced to think once more about the difference between patriotism and nationalism. Being not so much about knowing who we are but knowing who we're not, I had never had to think about it very hard before. If asked, I'd mumble something about being born in London and having Scottish grandparents living in Scotland, and move on. It takes someone else to waken the dragon lurking within and spark the embers of latent patriotism. And Northern Ireland had shown me that it doesn't take much to achieve this.

Can you be one and not the other? Albert Einstein and George Orwell certainly thought so. Einstein said 'Nationalism is an infantile sickness; the measles of the human race.' Orwell defined nationalism as 'loyalty to any cause or group, be it creed, race or country that recognises no other duty than the advancement of its own interests.'

Both contrasted this with patriotism which they felt represented a devotion to a particular place or way of life without any feeling of having to force it on others. The nationalist wants to secure power and prestige for whatever causal entity they have sunk their individual identity into and will often be willing to do whatever it takes to get their way. Where patriotism doesn't seem to need an enemy, nationalism seems to demand one. It is exclusive, not inclusive. And it's especially dangerous when whole countries become blinded by an ideology.

'Nationalism,' said Orwell, 'is inseparable from the desire for power. The abiding purpose of every nationalist is to secure more power and more prestige, not for himself but for the nation or group in which he has chosen to sink his own individuality.'

George Orwell was very clear in his distinctions between patriotism and nationalism. To Orwell, nationalism is the attitude by which whole groups of people label each other as 'good' or 'bad'. To identify oneself within a specific group—a nation, class, religion, movement or political grouping—was, he argued, to place oneself beyond good and evil.

Nationalism can define itself as being against a group. 'But patriotism,' says Orwell, 'is slightly different in as much that it infers devotion to a particular place, a particular way of life, which one believes to be the best in the world, but which one has no wish to force on other people. Patriotism is of its nature defensive, both militarily and culturally. Nationalism, on the other hand, is inseparable from the desire for power. The abiding purpose of every nationalist is to secure more power and more prestige, not for himself but for the nation or group in which he has chosen to sink his own individuality.'

So, there it was: It was either all about 'the nation', or it wasn't. But Yugoslavia, like so many federations, was something of a false construct, glued together in the wake of the Second World War by the idealistic bonds of communism and little else. Slovenia, Croatia, Serbia, Montenegro, Macedonia, and, to an extent, Bosnia and Hercegovina had existed long before Yugoslavia came about. Like most other nations, they had existed for centuries.

The former-Yugoslav republics were coming out of 45 years of communist rule, which had largely eliminated income inequalities. Throughout this period, no individual had been allowed to hold more than 10 hectares of land. More general indicators of income inequality suggest that income distributions were fairly equal prior to the 1990 elections, comparable to countries such as Sweden and Norway that have some of the most equitable income distributions in the world. Nevertheless income inequality was used as an issue to mobilise the population, especially by the Croats who resented profits from the cash-cow that was the Dalmatian tourist coast being spent in Serbia.

The Communist period did more, though, not only by diminishing the importance of class distinctions through income but by secularising society in such a way that it removed any potential for a significant sectarian cleavage. During the Communist period, Yugoslavia banished religious instruction from schools and strictly limited and monitored the activities of religious organisations, leaving most people sceptical of the role of religion in Yugoslav politics. Literacy rates were some of the highest in Europe, at 99% for those between the ages of 10 and 34. Urban centres consisted of small to medium-sized towns that were connected to surrounding villages by virtue of the fact that almost every family owned a 'veekend-iza', a small plot of land with a small bungalow where generally literate people could divide their time between their urban-based jobs and a bucolic rural idyl which allowed them to tend a small plot of their own land at weekends. Usually this involved the growing of grapes and the distillation of that staple of the Yugoslav diet, Ŝlivovića (plum brandy).

Once it had been grasped by a stunned Europe in the early 19th century that the divine rule of emperors and kings was coming to an end, the concept of nationhood began to gain legitimacy. The concept was built on three philosophical pillars:

The first is that legitimacy is derived from the people, and is not handed down from above. Philosophers like Rousseau and Locke drew on a well-established sense of national cause to explain how individual citizens have the right to join freely in a nation whose sole purpose is to protect and benefit them. Authority stems directly from the nation, they said.

The second is that government is not just an agreement between individuals, but also a statement of the general will. Yes, the individual can have rights, but so can the collective. Britain's Magna Carta was an early example of this. Sadly, however, governments have used and abused the principal ever since.

Third, and most important of all, is the assumption that each nation is somehow different. By the time Napoleon was invading his neighbours, France's claim to be spreading the universal virtues of liberty, fraternity, and equality looked to the rest of Europe very much like a brazen land-grab. The great thinkers of the day insisted that true nations are shaped by their own unique past, and that the true essence of each emerges from history, culture, language, and, ultimately, race.

Nationalism slips and slithers between these four complementary, yet divergent claims. Here, in a tiny and long forgotten sliver of muddy flood-plain on the banks of the River Danube proud to call itself Slavonia, decent people had turned, apparently overnight, into bigots, clinging blindly to a faith in their own nation's superiority. That nation was Croatia. But they were Slavonians first, Croats second. 'We were never Slavs, far less Yugoslavs,' they would snarl with contempt while downing yet another slivoviça to keep out the cold.

But one person's patriotic pride is another's nationalistic prejudice.

The manipulation of history and culture has a long tradition, with the process of national construction often being harnessed for violence and hatred. When Italy was unified in 1861, less than 3% of the population spoke Italian. At the time, Massimo d'Azeglio, a leading patriot, declared, 'We have made Italy, now we must make Italians.' So much for communities bound by language and culture. This journey has been described as one that 'starts with folk-dancing and ends up with barbed wire.'

Such journeys are apparently all too easy, especially when nationalism is contaminated by theories of racial purity. It was precisely this logic that justified the Nazis' drive to 'protect' ethnic Germans in neighbouring countries in the late 1930s, a drive that expanded to include the building of concentration camps and gas chambers. You would think that Croatia, being one of those 'neighbouring countries', had learned the lesson. Just the week before in the Bosnian town of Bihac—another ethnic enclaves that was to be later caught up in the bloodletting—I had been shown the unrepaired bullet holes in the walls of the Dom Stravija[17], put there in 1943 as the Wehrmacht retreated from Croatia in the face of the Allies' advance. Here I was, less than 50 years later, seeing history repeat itself.

How depressing, I thought to myself, as the far-off crump of incoming artillery shells began their nightly shower of death and destruction.

Perhaps our own imperial past might have something to do with it, I mused to myself, as the intermittent shelling crept closer. The British Empire could only stop itself from collapsing under the weight of its own contradictions by impressing upon their imperial subjects that they had not yet earned their right to an autonomous existence. Once this myth was exposed for what it was, the Empire collapsed.

Yet Canada—whose prairies are used by the British to practice their war games at a place called BATUS outside Calgary, and whose rolling grassy plains I had once driven my tank over—seemed to embrace each other's differences alright,

17. Health Centre

I thought. Indeed, a beer-swilling Canadian railway worker—whose job, incidentally, was to scare hibernating bears out of railway tunnels—once told me that Canadians had to work together to survive the cold winters. Québec, where years of anti-French prejudice eventually led to a powerful drive for independence, obliged them to accept that there is room for more than one culture on equal terms. It didn't take them long to celebrate their cultural differences and embrace an all-enveloping tolerance. For Canadians, nationalism was not a choice between cultural exceptionalism and moral universalism, but a benign and pragmatic mix of both. Why could these two men, who so clearly hated each other, not do the same?

But, although I was contracted by the British Foreign and Commonwealth Office, the FCO, I wasn't here as a Brit, but as a European. The armband and the baseball cap I was wearing were blue with 12 gold stars, the symbol of the most ambitious project ever attempted to lay nationalism to rest, the European Union. The irony of the situation was beginning to dawn on me. As the chaos grew, so did the equally firm conviction that only a strong ethnic culture and a powerful government could keep them safe. These people, the backbone of the new nationalism erupting around me, still secretly hoped, though, that the European Union would come galloping over the horizon to their rescue. How tragically misguided they were.

Only the day before, as I hunkered in a frontline bunker with a motely rag-tag collection of Croat soldiers, most of them wearing sneakers and any item of camouflaged clothing they had been able to scrounge, the banter had been of 'kućkin Četnika'[18] and how Milošević , their leader, was nothing more than a deluded maniac. But there had also been much mention of economics, of how Serbia was 'sucking the glorious motherland (Croatia) dry'. The Dalmatian coast, with the cities of Split and Dubrovnik lying like jewels in a crown of turquoise sea was, they knew, the key to their future prosperity, and they were damned if any Serb was going to plunder such jewels ever again. Tank parts being exported to Croatia was a symbol of this inequity. 'It's our sweat spilled on the factory floor, but it's those bastards who reap the reward.' Everywhere I went, I heard the same thing. To an outsider like me, it seemed that the root of this new nationalism was as much to do with economic inequity as it was to do with nationalistic ideology.

They perceived 'the system' to be rigged against them. Their hard work—real or imagined—had gone unrewarded while the self-serving elite in Belgrade and the Slavic minorities who enjoyed their favour reaped privileged access to wealth and power. No more. Power-hungry politicians obsessed with imagined wrongs which stretched back for generations gave jobs to their friends, while their own loyalty to the Yugoslav experiment had been rewarded with sneering derision and disdain.

---

18. pronounced 'kooch-kin chet-neeka' and means 'Serb bastards'

This flare-up of rampant nationalism did not just insist on the difference between socialism and capitalism, between Yugoslavia and the rest of the world—they were not blind; they had seen the Berlin Wall come down just three years earlier—but was thriving on the angry frustrations simmering within them. And it wasn't just Serbia and Croatia, Slovenia and Bosnia, it was Slavonia and Dalmatia too. States within states within states, each with their own legitimate claims to self-determination. But was the driving force for this explosion of hostility poverty, pride or power? Or was it something more elemental… the ability to control your own way of life, your own destiny?

As a political doctrine, nationalism is the belief that the world's peoples are divided into nations, and that each of these nations has an absolute right to self-determination. As a cultural ideal, nationalism is the claim that while people may have many identities, it is the nation, the motherland, that provides them with their primary form of belonging. As a moral ideal, nationalism is an ethic of heroic sacrifice, justifying the use of violence in defence of one's nation against enemies, internal or external. These claims—political, moral, and cultural—were feeding off each other. The moral claim that nations are entitled to be defended by force depends on the cultural claim that the needs they satisfy for security and belonging are uniquely important. The political idea that all peoples should struggle for nationhood depends on the cultural claim that only nations can satisfy these needs. And the cultural idea underwrites the political claim that these needs cannot be satisfied without self-determination. As Michael Ignatieff points out in his book *Blood and Belonging*, each of these claims is contestable. It is not obvious why national identity should be a more important element of personal identity than any other; nor is it obvious why its defence justifies the use of violence.

The fact that two Serbs share Serbian ethnic identity may unite them against Croats, but it can do nothing to stop them fighting each other over jobs, resources, spouses, and so on. A shared ethnicity, by itself, creates neither social cohesion nor community, and when it fails to do so—as it must—nationalist agendas are necessarily impelled toward maintaining unity by force, rather than by consent. This explains why nationalistic regimes are more authoritarian than democratic.

The fundamental appeal of ethnic nationalism is as a rationale for ethnic majority rule, for keeping one's enemies in their place, or for overturning some—often imagined—legacy of cultural subordination.

Faced with a situation of political and economic chaos, people want to know whom to trust and whom to call their own. Ethnic nationalism provides an intuitive answer: only trust those of your own blood. All this is mixed up with sentimental notions of fate and destiny. A love greater than reason helps in making frightened people believe that it is fate, however tragic, that obliges them to kill. If nationalism is persuasive because it warrants violence, it is also persuasive because it offers protection from violence. This is how everything gets turned on its head.

According to Michael Bilewicz, a social psychologist at the University of Warsaw, 'nationalism is determined not by patriotic ardour, but by self-esteem.' This suggests that loyalty to the nation, when combined with confidence and trust, favours altruism. By contrast, feelings of frustration and inadequacy tend to lead to narcissism. Those who, for whatever reason, feel disenfranchised look to 'the mother nation' to re-assure them that, in their own way, they are as good as everyone else. Even better, perhaps. If the world does not accord them the respect they feel they deserve, they are quick to identify with those who share their insecurities, and show contempt for others. Was this what is was all about? A national inferiority complex on the part of the Croats?

Altruists acknowledge their chequered past, give thanks for today's blessings, and look forward to a better future for them and their children. Narcissists with an inferiority complex, on the other hand, exalt in the largely mythological glories of the past, denigrate a miserable present, and promise a magnificent future. A new dawn. Less than fifty years before, Hitler and Mussolini had stoked nationalist fears on just this premise in two countries lying close by to North and West, Italy and Austria. And fifty years is not long enough for memory and resentment to fade.

The belief that nationalism would fade away in the communist utopia of post-war Yugoslavia, was always naïve. The only question was what form it would take. As I cowered in that bunker, drinking hot tea and fresh doughnuts with a group of muddied and bloodied fanatics, and with Serb snipers pointing rifles at me from not more than 200 metres away, I was finding out for myself the answer to that question.

LEGACY

LOOKING BACK, IT MAY well be that post-war ethnic cleansing re-emerged in all its horror in Vukovar, on the banks of the mighty Danube. But back in the early winter of 1991, such incidents appeared to be isolated; there was no evidence of organised, systemic, or widespread application.

Yes, Vukovar was the first town in Europe to suffer complete devastation since the Second World War, and Yes the pattern of siege and indiscriminate bombardment of civilians that later characterised the Yugoslav wars, was first seen there. But in this, the siege of Vukovar was, at the time anyway, just another war crime.

Yet, as former BBC reporter Martin Bell pointed out at the time, 'The siege also paved the way for a new and terrible phrase to enter into common usage. The first case of organised terrorism—later to be known as ethnic cleansing—took place in Vukovar when over 200 wounded soldiers, volunteers, and nursing staff were rounded up, sent to a remote farmhouse, tortured, shot, and dumped in a mass grave.'

But none of us knew that then.

The Battle of Vukovar was an 87-day siege of a mid-sized market town in eastern Croatia by the Yugoslav People's Army (JNA), supported by various paramilitary forces from Serbia, between August and November 1991. Before the Croatian War of Independence the Baroque town was a prosperous, mixed community of Croats, Serbs and other ethnic groups. As Yugoslavia began to break up, Serbia's President Slobodan Milošević and Croatia's President Franjo Tuđman began pursuing nationalist politics. In 1990, an armed insurrection was started by Croatian Serb militias, supported by the Serbian government and paramilitary groups, who seized control of Serb-populated areas of Croatia.

Serb propaganda portrayed Croatian separatists as genocidal Ustaše[19] who had illegally taken over Yugoslav territory and were threatening Serb civilians in a reprise of the anti-Serb pogroms of the Second World War.

The JNA began to intervene in favour of the rebellion, and conflict broke out in the eastern Croatian region of Slavonia in May 1991. The JNA responded by launching a major offensive

19. pronounced 'Oostasha'

in eastern Slavonia, from where it intended to progress west via Vinkovci and Osijek to Zagreb. Vukovar was the main focus of the offensive, but, as happened with Stalingrad in the Second World War, an initially inconsequential engagement became an essential political symbol for both sides.

Vukovar was defended by around 1,800 lightly armed Croatian soldiers and civilian volunteers, against as many as 36,000 JNA soldiers and Serb paramilitaries equipped with heavy armour and artillery. During the battle, shells and rockets were fired into the town at a rate of up to 12,000 a day. At the time, it was the fiercest and most protracted battle seen in Europe since 1945, and Vukovar was the first major European town to be entirely destroyed since the Second World War. When Vukovar fell on 18 November 1991, several hundred soldiers and civilians were massacred by Serb forces and at least 20,000 inhabitants were expelled. Most of Vukovar was ethnically cleansed of its non-Serb population and became part of the self-declared Republic of Serbian Krajina. Several Serb military and political officials, including Milošević, were later indicted and in some cases jailed for war crimes committed during and after the battle.

Around 400 people from Vukovar's hospital—non-Serb patients, medical personnel, local political figures and others who had taken refuge there—were taken by the JNA. Although some were subsequently released, around 200 were transported to the nearby Ovčara farm and executed in what became known as the Vukovar massacre. At least 50 others were taken elsewhere and never seen again. Thousands more were transferred to prison camps in Serbia and rebel-controlled Croatia. Further mass killings followed.

The international community made repeated unsuccessful attempts to end the fighting. Both sides violated ceasefires, often within hours. Calls by some European Community members for the Western European Union to intervene militarily were vetoed by the United Kingdom. Instead, a Conference for Yugoslavia was established under the chairmanship of Lord Carrington to find a way to end the conflict. The United Nations (UN) imposed an arms embargo on all of the Yugoslav republics in September 1991 under Security Council Resolution 713, but this was ineffective, in part because the JNA had no need to import weapons. The European powers abandoned attempts to keep Yugoslavia united and agreed to recognise the independence of Croatia and Slovenia on 15 January 1992.

ECMM monitors tried unsuccessfully to prevent the human rights abuses that followed the battle. A visit by UN envoys Marrack Goulding and Cyrus Vance was systematically obstructed by the JNA. Vance's demands to see the hospital, from which wounded patients were being dragged out to be killed, were rebuffed by one of the massacre's chief architects who blocked Red Cross representatives in an angry confrontation recorded by TV cameras: 'This is my country, we have conquered this. This is Yugoslavia, and I am in command here!'

Following the battle, Vukovar became a symbol of Croatian resistance and suffering. For their part, many individual JNA soldiers who took part in the battle were revolted by what they had seen and protested to their superiors about the behaviour of the paramilitaries. Colonel Milorad Vučić later commented that 'they simply do not want to die for such things'. The atrocities that they witnessed led some to experience subsequent feelings of trauma and guilt, with one JNA veteran later telling a journalist, 'I was in the Army and I did my duty. Vukovar was more of a slaughter than a battle. Many women and children were killed. Many, many.'

Signs of the battle are still widely apparent in Vukovar, where many buildings remain visibly scarred by bullets and shrapnel. The riverside water tower has been preserved in its badly damaged state as a memorial. The town hospital presents an exhibition and reconstruction of the conditions in the building during the battle. At Ovčara, the site of the massacre is marked by a mass grave and exhibition about the atrocity. Local guides, some of whom lived through the battle, offer tourists the opportunity to visit these and other sites on walking and bicycle tours.

Years later, while touring the old battle grounds, I shared a coffee with one of the guides. This was all he would say about those days:

'The futility of it all was that I picked up a gun without even really knowing what the prize was. Not that it mattered much because in the semi-drunken, drugged-up state we call war, and however befuddled, the battle to survive takes over. Kill or be killed. That's all any of us really knew. Fighting knows only itself. It mutates into a self-fulfilling form of morbid competition which goes on and on until, one day, it ends. Just like that. Silence. And it ends for everyone, and in the same way... with bitterness and exhaustion and having spawned yet more generations who will know only suffering, vengeance and recrimination.'

This is the legacy of Vukovar, and it was into this profound feeling of despair that I arrived in Vinkovci, a border town just visible to the South, less than three months later.

ORIGINS

THE NIGHT WAS BLACK and damp. Between the explosive crumps, some close, some far away, I heard souls being sucked up through the muffled snowy silence like the last drops of a milk-shake being sucked up through a straw. It was the sound of desolation. And the silence that followed was deafening me.

I had been trying to snatch some sleep between the intermittent artillery barrages in the freezing basement gym of Vinkovci's only habitable hotel metres from what the Croats referred to as 'The Eastern Front'

Sleeping on a bench in a hotel's basement gym is a sensible thing to do when on the receiving end of an artillery barrage. But it doesn't make for a good night's sleep, especially when one's ears are still ringing from when the Colonel shot the lock off the door with his Colt-45 only a few hours earlier.

It was the silence that woke me. That, and being shaken by Dünya.

'Gospodin James,' she hissed in my ear. 'You have to come with me... !'

'Dünya, it's four o'clock in the morning... what on earth are you doing?'

'It's the Colonel. He wants to show you something.'

Stumbling upstairs, my head-torch lighting the way, I found the Colonel talking into his VHF handheld radio in the hotel lobby. 'Da. He is here. We are coming!'

'Colonel, *Dober dan*. What's going on? You know ECMM monitors are not allowed out at night...'

'I will explain in the car,' is all he said in reply and steered me out into the chill dark night. A soft snow was falling.

With whispered apologies from our Croatian liaison officer, Major Matić, we were bundled into a camouflaged Mercedes jeep and driven off, no lights showing, into the night. A light snow was beginning to settle on the piles of rubble and blackened beams piled up along the roadside, all that remained of Vinkovci's blasted suburbs.

After half-an-hour or so of jolting along icy country tracks, we drew up behind a row of buses each of which had their headlights on and pointing towards the Serb frontline. In front of me a bright red and yellow sign swung from a single strand of barbed wire. 'Achtung! Minen!' it declared.

We were standing on the edge of a front-line minefield, fully exposed to Serb snipers lurking unseen in the darkness.

I turned to Major Matić in search of some explanation. All he did was point across No-Man's land.

Emerging into the pool of light, a dozen dim shapes stumbled into view.

There was no sound. No sound at all. The sort of muffled silence one hears only when it is snowing. I observed this macabre spectacle from a safe distance as if it were a scene in a grainy black and white film from the 1950's with the sound turned off. It was the scene of my nightmare.

As the huddled figures drew closer, I began to make out details. There were no men. Only children, mothers and grandmothers. Every single one had bloodstained ears. I learned later this was because they had just had their gold ear-rings ripped out. Not taken out. Ripped out.

There was no crying, no sobbing. In fact, not a word was spoken. From their blank, hollow-eyed expressions they were in shock. Through the swirling snow, more figures emerged. And in one's and two's they kept on coming.

I didn't know it then, but I was witnessing the first recorded act of a new policy not seen in Europe since the end of the Second World War, 'Ethnic Cleansing.' It was shocking in its brutality. And it defied everything I thought I knew about the human condition, something that became much clearer to me when Dünya and I were driven to the local gymnasium to see these pathetic shivering victims of Serb atrocity being processed.

Dünya translated some of their testimonies. Most were too awful to repeat but included stories of grandmothers being beheaded with rusty saws and the gang-rape of young girls.

Still in shock myself, I sat on the floor and wrote a hurried report to ECMM headquarters in Zagreb describing what I had witnessed.

A few hours later, numb and exhausted from seeing and hearing what was going on around me, I received a phone call from my boss at ECMM headquarters in Zagreb telling me to return at once. Since this involved an eight-hour drive via Hungary and Slovenia, I made my excuses, went back to the hotel in Vinkovci to collect my equipment, and set off.

Thinking that the reason for my recall was connected with the sordid details outlined in my report, I made good time, arriving at the Hotel-i on the south bank of the Sava river outside Zagreb in my canvas-sided, mud-spattered white Jeep just as the sun was setting. It didn't take long for me to realise that my report had not even been read, far less acted upon. I had been recalled for more mundane reasons. As one of only five native English-speakers in the entire mission, I had to replace the duty analyst who had been taken ill. No mention was made of my report, despite having sent it as a 'flash update' approximately eight hours earlier. I tried to raise the issue with the UK delegate, but was waved away. After a quick shower and even quicker briefing, I was shown to a small room above the front door in what used to be the hotel's travel bureau where I was to spend the night collating, interpreting and summarising the daily situation reports (SitReps) from each of the 42 ECMM monitoring teams stationed along the 528 km-long demarcation line between Croatia and its Serbian, Montenegrin and Bosnian neighbours.

Although interesting, this long and tedious job meant working through the night in order to provide a written and oral briefing to the ECMM's assembled heads of mission at 07:30 the next morning. Given that I'd only had a few hours' sleep the night before—much of it interrupted by sporadic artillery fire—the traumas of my early morning spent bearing witness in the frozen wastelands of East Slavonia, and the long bumpy journey, I was not in the most energetic frame of mind. But I was under no illusion as to how important the job was.

Almost immediately the messages started coming through on the CapSat[20]. One of the first was my own sent earlier that morning. It seemed a lifetime ago, and I had to read it twice to be reminded of the full horror of what the dry words rather dispassionately described.

As the night wore on, the roll of incoming messages being spewed out from the printer grew longer and longer. They arrived in no particular order which meant that I had to locate the team

20. At the time, 'CapSat' was a new, mobile, satellite-based system for transmitting encrypted written messages over long distances by radio.

sending it on the wall-map behind me before I could make sense of the places they were referring to. As I read through each one, it became increasingly clear that I had not been alone in witnessing the aftermath of true barbarity just over 24 hours before; each SitRep outlined similarly gruesome stories from towns and villages all along the ceasefire line. Each case involved Croats being forcibly expelled from disputed areas by Serb or Bosnian Serb regular and irregular forces.

By 2 o'clock in the morning it was very clear that these were no random acts of violence and that we were witnessing an ugly shift in policy, this time on the part of the Serbs. It was even pretty clear that there was an element of command and control which had hitherto been unseen, and that this could not have come from the capital of the self-proclaimed province of *Republika Srpska* in Banja Luka, but from the very top in Belgrade. If true, this was a game-changer. I rushed upstairs to wake my now seriously-ill colleague, Barney Mayhew, who was able to confirm that this was indeed something new.

As I painstakingly compiled the evidence in support of my analysis, my thoughts turned to how best to describe what was going on. Having been an advertising executive for some years after leaving the military, I looked around for words that were rational yet emotive, truthful yet evocative. This was not a report to be ignored. With less than an hour to go before briefing the assembled diplomats, I was left with just the executive summary to complete. I had already determined that the mass expulsions the monitoring teams had been witnessing over the past 24 hours did not constitute 'genocide' and, while not solely driven by ethnicity, the practice seemed to me to be determined more by this aspect than by religion, class, language or ideology. Either way, I needed a verb.

Huddled in the Hotel-i, one of the few forms of distraction was to read week-old copies of newspapers which various delegations left strewn about once they had read them themselves. Idly flicking through them just a few hours earlier, I had noticed that the UK tabloids were full of Princess Diana's marriage problems and how she had taken to colonic irrigation as a form of therapy. This form of anal cleansing apparently involved inserting a tube into the rectum and flushing out excreta from the lower intestine with warm salty water, a process which seemed to me to be a rather dirty way of achieving a clean result. Purging by enema. This was certainly a more apt description of what I had been witnessing these past few days in East Slavonia than 'cleaning', with its image of soft hands and sparkling dishes. I toyed for a few moments with 'ethnic enema' but thought the alliteration too facile. Anyway, it lacked a verb so implied no action. Purging was useful but had probably been used before. So 'cleansing' it was.

I had enough evidence to determine that what was going on was systemic and centrally controlled. What I couldn't deduce from the reports, though, was the underlying cause. Was this barbaric form of nationalism motivated by history or mythology? By politics or economics?

Was it sectarian or racial? Or was it not driven by idealism at all, but by jealousy and a thirst for revenge? I couldn't decide. Was it like Northern Ireland, where so much of what was painted as sectarian strife was in fact nothing more than low-level banditry based on theft, smuggling, and the settling of local grudges by various factions and criminal gangs.

These thoughts and many others raced through my mind as the clock ticked down. I was still agonising over which words to use when the first tendrils of dawn crept into the night sky over the Sava river flowing past my office window.

The briefing was designed to shock, and shock it did. Every one of the ambassadors representing their country's contribution to the ECMM was present and understood full well the importance of what they had just heard. Had this been an act of genocide, I could hear them thinking, their countries would have been compelled to do more than monitor; they would have had to take preventive action, something the European Community was woefully ill-prepared for. After some discussion over whether or not the term was overly emotive—in which I argued that it was not hyperbole but a careful construction based on solid analysis of compelling evidence—my report was sent to the European Commission's headquarters in Brussels more or less as I had written it, from where it was more widely distributed (in the form of a COREU[21]) to the capitals of Europe. Less than 24 hours later it was used in an official briefing by the Croatian representative of the United Nations High Commissioner for Refugees, José-Maria Mendiluce, with whom it had been shared, and the next morning it was plastered over the world's front pages[22].

But on what basis had I come to the conclusions I had? I was not a human rights lawyer, so how had I determined that what we were witnessing along the *Krajina* border was something other than genocide?

---

21. COREU - Correspondance Européenne—is a communication network of the European Council for diplomatic communications to and from foreign ministries of member states of the European Union.
22. José-Maria went on to claim that it was he who had 'invented' the term.

UNDERLYING CAUSES

LIKE MY FELLOW monitors, I had thought long and hard since my arrival in former-Yugoslavia about what was unfolding around me. I had met enough Serbs, Croats and Bosnians over the preceding weeks to know that each had competing—and, to them, compelling—claims over history and truth. Don't we all? But the stories I kept hearing seemed to be re-writing nearly fifty years of multicultural co-existence, reframing it in a simplistic narrative of heroic suffering and national victimisation. While the soldiers protecting me were certain of their cause in an unstable world, I wondered how they held their world together in the face of competing socio-economic status, family relations, and religious belief. The sense of victimisation and suffering being deployed by their political leaders had become a form of moral asset. Overall, the grand narrative was one of historical injustice, subordination, and exploitation. Listening to such rhetoric while huddling around wood-burning stoves in front-line bunkers with young Croat conscripts in places like Pakrac, Duga Resa and Vinkovci, I remember thinking that there must have been equally young and idealistic Serbs not more than a few hundred metres away thinking much the same.

I had only been in Croatia for a few weeks, but already I was getting a sense of where the Croats were coming from. Their recent harrowing experiences combined with this trope of victimisation was being manipulated as a vehicle for nationalist propaganda and as a rhetorical device for pointing the finger of blame at the crimes of others in order to elude or elide accountability for wrongs of their own doing. Being a monitor from the European Community, I had to remain neutral and impartial, but it was clear to all of us that it wasn't just the Serbs that were culpable.

Nevertheless, it was made clear to us at every turn that the palpable sense of superiority on the part of the Croats stemmed in large measure from their understanding of themselves as guardians of Europe and a bulwark of Christianity. This rather narcissistic view apparently dated from the Ottoman invasion of the 16th century. Given that rule by Venice and Constantinople was followed by Habsburg dominance and later replaced by a centralised Yugoslav administration established after the Second World War, the fact that they imagined themselves to be under a constant state of threat and victimisation was perhaps understandable. In their view, their ancestors had successfully protected the borders of Europe against intruding forces 'from the East'. In the popular imagination, no other historical event or encounter is considered more significant for the formation of national identity and self-conception than the various battles against the forces of the Ottoman Empire which took place along the Krajina frontier throughout 1715. These gave rise to a rich repertoire of folk ballads, tales, proverbs, and songs which provide the founding myth on which local codes of honour, morality, and heroism had been built. It is this founding myth which allowed Croats to perceive themselves as the last bastion of defence against Islamic intrusion.

This theme typically expressed itself as a complaint that their historic role was not being adequately acknowledged. The fact that I, a foreigner and representative of the European Community, was in the room with them was probably the first time they felt they were being taken seriously and that the world was listening. They weren't. Recognition by Germany just months earlier had given them false hope and, with it, a false sense of the righteousness of their cause.

That a great convulsion was to shake East Slavonia in the winter of 1991/92 came as no great surprise given the fanaticism with which such beliefs were held. A festering slurry of land disputes, ethnic identity, economic inequality, and post-imperial collapse was a potent brew waiting only to be stirred by the ladle of post-war demographics and ignited by the distrust and fear of modern politics. This was, after all, the land where there were people still alive who remembered the assassination of Franz Ferdinand in Sarajevo in 1916 as if it were yesterday and who recalled the endless Nazi massacres of the Second World War as if it was this morning. Certainly, there were plenty of old people around who could testify to atrocities committed by the Nazis, their Croatian puppets, the Ustaše[23], Tito's Partisans, and/or the Četniks[24]. Old enmities run deep when history is real and not something you learn about only in school.

Whole peoples are shaped by their history, of course: The English by Agincourt; the Scots by Bannockburn; the Americans by Gettysburg; the Serbs by Kosovo Polje; and, more recently, the Croats by Vukovar. Each nation, each people, deserve their foundational myth. But some myths are more sacred than others—as Kosovo Polje, for example, is to the Serbs—with most being shaped more by blood than by geography, most of it in a form that nowadays would be referred to as genocidal.

---

23. A Croatian ultra-nationalist and fascist organisation led by Ante Pavelić—the uncle of one of my interpreters—and active between 1929 and 1945.
24. A network of Serb nationalists who came to prominence in Yugoslavia during WWII and whose vision of an ethnically homogeneous Greater Serbian state was advanced by an opportunistic policy of collaboration with the Axis (Germand and Italian) forces. Usually heavily bearded and wearing the astrakan Šubara cap.

Dünya and her fellow interpreters had grown up during a time when one national myth was being replaced by another. The old Yugoslavia that was swept away in the early 1990's had been founded during the Second World War when the struggle against fascism was shared by all ethnic groups. Its national moto was 'Brotherhood and Unity'. This was a story to unite all those who lived in the Federal Republic of Yugoslavia, Serb, Croat and Bosniak alike.

The communist wartime leader, Josip Tito died in 1980 and, in the decade that followed, the story of a peaceful, multi-ethnic state at ease with itself began to give way to something else.

The shift was subtle and insidious. Slowly but surely, as the decade proceeded, a quasi-religious millennial liberation narrative came to fore which positioned Serbs as a persecuted group going back to the Ottoman period; a group which had, in their telling, heroically defended Christendom against the rise of the Turk, and which had managed to preserve their language, history and religion over many centuries of Ottoman despotism.

By the end of the decade, every communist regime in Europe except that in Serbia had been toppled by populist uprisings. In Serbia, Milošević alone held on to power. He cemented that power by applying a potent mix of history, political theatre and ritual. In June 1989, as this series of democratic revolutions approached their zenith and the Berlin wall was about to fall, Milošević addressed a huge rally of fellow Serbs in their heartland of Kosovo. The occasion was the 600th anniversary of the infamous Battle of Kosovo Polje in 1389, the battle at which the medieval Serbian kingdom was defeated by an Ottoman army, ushering in centuries of Ottoman occupation across Serbia. Over the roar of tens of thousands of his fellow Serbs, he said that here they were once again, six hundred years later, once again engaged in an existential battle against a similar threat. The story resonated powerfully across Serbia and in those parts of Bosnia inhabited by ethnic Serbs who felt especially vulnerable. In hindsight, this speech demonstrated the beginnings of the process by which long-dormant ethnic enmity could be stoked.

Tensions of the past re-surface to challenge identity. Working with history, or representations of history often only loosely connected with reality, is a critical tool of identity politics. Collective hate is a product of organisation and mobilisation of groups. Milošević and later, the Bosnian Serb leader Radovan Karadic, argued that Serbs were once again facing the threat of extermination and that they had a duty to take up the heroic struggle for national unity and self-determination that had begun six centuries earlier. The message was clear: If you want to resist occupation and persecution you must be the one to initiate violence. Violence, said Karadic, is a unifying right and providence called for a 'necessary baptism by blood.'

As in Rwanda a few years later, religion was not left out. The Serbs would prevail, he said, because they are defined by their orthodox

Christian faith. The Serbs had saved medieval Christian Europe from the Ottoman Turks. Any war would be a holy war. Liberation thus becomes intertwined with religion. It didn't take much imagination to see Muslims reconceptualised as Turks; not as neighbours and the fellow citizens they had been for hundreds of years but the living embodiment of Ottoman oppression.

It was very obvious to any outside observer with eyes to see in early 1992 that a shift in popular sentiment was accelerating and that long-held conceptions of 'who we are' no longer matched 'who we might become.' Propaganda was seeping in to contaminate the groundwater of public perception. Teachers, Doctors and Civil Servants began to ask ever-more personal questions about parentage, ethnicity, social class, and worship. Slowly but surely they too were becoming 'middle managers of ethnic cleansing' and began to turn rhetoric into a real and local reality.

The project of 'ethnic cleansing' was pursued systematically municipality by municipality. Although not so obvious in its earlier guises, the strategy was centrally directed. It was a top-down, state-sponsored project. Many of those who wittingly or unwittingly took part said later that they should have seen the signs, and that, had they done so, they would have taken action to stop matters from spiralling out of control. Nazi prison camp guards said much the same. I was there. I saw what was going on. And, if it was obvious to me, it must have been doubly so to them.

The genocide as represented by the massacres at Srebrenica marked an escalation from the strategy of 'ethnic cleansing' that predated it. The change of gear forced the hand of an anguished world.

Tragically—and perhaps inevitably—the legacy endures. The Serbian struggle of the 1990's remains a central part of an emerging heroic narrative of the global far right today. The poetry and music of that struggle inspires groups like Islamic State and was even playing in the car of the man who murdered over fifty people, including women and children, in cold blood in Christchurch, New Zealand in March 2019 as he drove to the scene. This is the soundtrack of hate and 'ethnic cleansing'. The manifestos of hate have migrated from the killing fields of Croatia to the internet forums of the far-right. As 9/11 made starkly clear, it turns out that ancient enmities are not so ancient after all and we are not as immune as we like to think.

This challenges us to think about where our loyalties lie. To family, clan, or country? Or to all of the above? The implication that you can't love your country without first loving the people you live amongst is all-pervading, eventually becoming so smothering that to live, even to breath, can mean only one thing: uncritical acceptance. The fear of 'other', of being cast out by the tribe, is a powerful, atavistic human urge in all of us. Put there by evolution, it reminds us that we are only human and must follow the herd too. After all, there's protection in numbers. Ask any shoaling fish being circled by a shark or herd of gazelle being stalked by a lion. Perhaps we shouldn't judge too harshly?

INTERNATIONAL LAW

WHEN ATTEMPTING TO post-rationalise my argument months later, I found out that the relationship between 'ethnic cleansing' as a policy and international laws of armed conflict in the broader sense is situated in the nexus between three legal constructs: the Geneva Conventions; Crimes Against Humanity; and Genocide. When the UN Security Council used the term for the first time in resolution 771 (1992) of 13 August 1992, it expressly stated that the practice violated international humanitarian law, but it didn't define how.

It was clear at the time that the more barbaric methods of ethnic cleansing constituted grave breaches of the 1949 Geneva Conventions and additional protocols of 1977. Even a superficial scan of the actions listed in the CapSat messages streaming in that night back in March supported this conclusion, and furthermore made it clear that there had been a distinction between individual criminality and systemic criminality.

It was equally clear that what had happened corresponded to crimes against humanity given that the ECMM teams were witnessing a systematic and wholesale attack on the civilian population. Whilst they were witnessing expulsion of targeted population groups from disputed territories, however, there was no evidence at the time that there was any intention to exterminate them.

But could extreme examples of the practice be described as genocide? At the time I thought not, though later events in Bosnia over the months and years which followed made me question this slightly rushed judgement.

The Genocide Convention defines genocide as the intentional destruction of a group of people, in whole or in part. In other words, genocide need not involve the destruction of an *entire* group and to differentiate it from other crimes against humanity it is necessary only to establish an *intent* to destroy. According to article 4 of the Statute of the International Tribunal for the former Yugoslavia of 1991, the crime of genocide must 'shock the conscience of mankind; result in great loss to humanity; be contrary to moral law and to the spirit and aims of the United Nations as per General Assembly Resolution 96 (1) of 11 December 1946.'

Remember, this was March 1992; Europe had not witnessed genocidal tendencies or ethnic cleansing since what Richard Evans called 'the expulsion under brutal and often murderous conditions of some 11 million ethnic Germans from Eastern Europe in 1944-46'[25] and the war in Bosnia-Herzegovina had not yet started. At the time, this was a war between Serbs and Croats—even though some of its effects were playing out in Bosnian territory and involved Bosnian Serbs and Bosnian Croats—and was not yet targeting Muslims specifically. Things had become much clearer by the end of the year—by which time the war in Bosnia was in full flow.

But the term still had to be described. What *was* 'ethnic cleansing' precisely? Like a great work of art, 'ethnic cleansing' defies easy definition; you know it when you see it. But, more importantly, you know what it's not. At least, I thought I did. As a soldier I had attended military law courses and knew roughly how 'genocide' was defined. As with war crimes,' ethnic cleansing' covers a wide range of sins, but extermination of entire groups of people was not one of them and was not what the ECMM monitoring teams or myself were witnessing. 'Ethnic cleansing' is about kicking people out, preferably permanently, but not their physical annihilation.

Although I was aware of the term 'genocide', I didn't know that it had only been invented in 1944 by a Polish lawyer, Raphael Lemkin. His

25. Evans: From Nazism to Never Again; Foreign Affairs, Jan/Feb 2018

definition, I knew, centred on a deliberate and intentional act perpetrated by the state to destroy an ethnic, national, or religious group. What I didn't know at the time was that the partial destruction of such a group legally constituted genocide as well. Nor did I know that genocide was aimed at wiping an entire people off the face of the planet, not just physically but also culturally. It was only some months later when I was in Banja Luka that I came across the deliberate destruction of mosques, libraries, and museums. And it was only when I was visiting Tuzla a couple of years later that it became clear that killing all male members of a particular ethnic group while leaving the women alive was also considered an act of genocide. It was certainly more than ethnic cleansing.

Years later, when reading Naomi Klein's terrifying book *The Shock Doctrine*, I realised I hadn't been alone is struggling with definitions. This is what she said on the subject:

> *In September 2006, twenty-three years after the end of Argentina's military dictatorship, one of the main enforcers of Pinochet's dictatorial reign of terror was finally sentenced to life in prison. The convicted man was Miguel Osvaldo Etchecolatz, former police commissioner of the province of Buenos Aires during the junta years.*
>
> *The judge in the case, fifty-five-year-old Carlos Rozanski of Argentina's federal court, found Etchecolatz guilty of six counts of homicide, six counts of unlawful imprisonment and seven cases of torture. When he handed down his verdict, he took an*

extraordinary step. He said that the conviction did not do justice to the true nature of the crime and that, 'in the interest of the construction of collective memory,' he needed to add that these were 'all crimes against humanity committed in the context of the genocide that took place in Republic of Argentina in 1976 and 1983.'

With that sentence, the judge played his part in the rewriting of Argentine history: the killings of leftists in the 70's were not part of a 'dirty war' in which two sides clashed and various crimes were committed, as had been the official story for decades. Nor were the disappeared merely victims of mad dictators who were drunk on sadism and their own personal power. What had happened was something more scientific, more terrifyingly rational. As the judge put it, there had been a 'plan of extermination carried out by those who ruled the country.'

He explained that the killings were part of a system, planned far in advance, duplicated in identical fashion across the country, and committed with clear intent, not of attacking individual persons but of destroying the parts of society that those people represented. In this sense, argued the judge, Pinochet's experiment with extreme capitalism ended up being genocidal in intent.

Rozanski recognised that his use of the word 'genocide' was controversial, and he wrote a lengthy piece backing up the choice. He acknowledged that the UN Convention on Genocide defines the crime as 'an intent to destroy, in whole or in part, a national, ethnic, religious or racial group'; the convention does not include eliminating a group based on its political beliefs—as had clearly been the case in Argentina—but the learned judge was of the opinion that he did not consider that exclusion to be legally legitimate. Pointing to a little-known chapter in UN history, he explained that on 11 December 1946, in direct response to the Nazi Holocaust, the UN General Assembly passed a resolution by unanimous vote barring acts of genocide 'when racial, religious, political and other groups have been destroyed, entirely or in part.' The reason the word 'political' had been excised from the convention two years later was that Stalin demanded it. He knew that if destroying a 'political group' for ideological reasons was genocidal, either in practice or in intent, his bloody purges and mass imprisonment of political opponents would qualify. Stalin had enough support from other leaders who also wanted to reserve the right to wipe out their political opponents that the word was discreetly dropped[26].

Rozanski wrote that he considered the original UN definition to be the more legitimate, since it had not been subject to this self-interested compromise. He noted that the criminal codes of many countries, including Portugal, Peru and Costa Rica, specifically bar acts of genocide, with definitions that clearly include 'political' and 'social' groups. French law, he also noted, was even broader, defining genocide as 'a plan intended to destroy in whole or in part a group determined by any arbitrary criteria.'

26. Van Schaack: The Crime of Political Genocide—Repairing the genocide Convention's blind spot; Yale Law Journal No.107 Vol.7, May 1997

> *He also made reference to a ruling by a Spanish National Court that had put one of Argentina's notorious torturers on trial in 1998. That court had also ruled that Argentina's military junta had committed the crime of genocide. It defined the group the junta was trying to wipe out as 'those citizens that did not fit the model determined by the repressors to be suitable for the new order being established in the country.' Like criminal courts before and since, it was trying to define which group had been targeted for extermination. 'The junta's goal,' wrote the presiding judge, Baltasar Garzon, 'was to establish a new order—like Hitler hoped to achieve in Germany—in which there was no room for certain types of people.'*

There is, of course, no comparison in scale between what happened under the Nazis or in Rwanda in 1994 and the dictatorships of Latin America in the 70's. If genocide means a holocaust, these crimes do not belong in that category. However, if genocide is understood as these courts were attempting to define it, as attempts to deliberately obliterate those groups who were barriers to a political project, then this process describes very well what was going on in former-Yugoslavia.

It wouldn't have mattered much if I had been aware of these distinctions, as what I and my fellow monitors had witnessed did not involve destruction, either in whole or in part. What it involved was the forced expulsion, not the mass slaughter, of the 'other' whoever they might be. But there was still no term I knew of that captured this difference.

None of this is to suggest that such disgusting practices were not to be found in the annals of human history long before this[27], merely that the term 'ethnic cleansing' had not been used to describe them, at least not in English. I was unaware, for example, that 'ethnic cleansing' can be a literal translation of the Serbo-Croat expression 'etničko čiŝćenje'. But as Drazen Petrovic points out in his book The *Roots of Ethnic Cleansing in Europe*, the origin of the term, even in its original language, is difficult to establish and that mass media reports discussed the establishment of 'ethnically clean territories' in Kosovo as far back as 1981.

But what's in a word? As the term began to gain traction in the media, reference was also made to 'ethnic purification', while the French often use the word 'nettoyage', which means 'cleaning', an altogether less brutal concept. Despite the fundamental difference between the English word 'cleansing'—which implies dirty means to achieve clean ends—and 'cleaning'—which implies clean means to achieve clean ends, rather like 'mild green fairy liquid' cleans dirty dishes—the words are often used as synonyms and therefore used interchangeably.

This random application of interchangeable words has only served to emphasise the unclear nature of the term itself which is why it is usually prefixed by the words 'so-called' or surrounded by parentheses.

---

27. Bell-Fialkoff: A Brief History of Ethnic Cleansing; Foreign Affairs, Vol.72, No.3, 1993

Furthermore, governments, international organisations, and non-governmental organisations have employed—some more deliberately than others—similarly diverse terminology. Ethnic cleansing is sometimes described as a systematic process, a pattern, a policy, or a practice. All this may at first glance seem insignificant but it actually indicates a substantial difference in attitude and intent. Such are the subtle vagaries of language.

As soon as the capitals of Europe realised the significance of the ECMM's COREU, I found myself having to defend my analysis. That something bestial was happening was self-evident, but the context was perhaps less so. Given what was going through my head at the time I framed my response in the form of a definition. It went something like this:

> *The specific, pre-determined and systematically applied political intent by a national authority or its agents to permanently alter the demography of a defined geographic area on the basis of ethnic, racial, linguistic, religious or other ideological and social criteria through the means of coerced expulsion, including terror.*

Notably absent from this definition was any reference to extermination or total physical destruction, and it was this element that I felt differentiated the practice of 'ethnic cleansing' from genocide. At the same time, any policy of 'ethnic cleansing'—for that is what it is, a policy—fundamentally represents a violation of human rights and international humanitarian law. While the individual methods applied appear to construe crimes against humanity, or even war crimes, 'ethnic cleansing' falls short of genocide as the intent to bring about the permanent destruction of any group perceived as being 'other' is not implied.

Crucially, the definition also included reference to 'pre-determined', 'systematic' and 'national'. This is because it was very clear to ECMM monitors that what they had witnessed in the six months prior to March 1992 amounted either to destruction of urban centres like Vukovar and the shelling of places like Dubrovnik or terrorisation of rural villages by marauding gangs of what were little more than spontaneous, home-grown gangster militias, and that these events in themselves did not amount to a policy. The term 'ethnic cleansing' was only coined once it became clear that what had started in East Slavonia and rippled along the length of the *Krajina* no longer constituted random acts of violence but the systematic application of terror planned, unleashed and controlled from the centre.

I didn't just have to defend my use of the words 'ethnic' and 'cleansing', either, but justify why I had paired them together. If the two words are themselves ambiguous—which they are—they are even more so when used together. My logic was very simple: In everyday use 'cleaning' evokes positive connotations of cleanliness, warm water and soapy bubbles, even purity and chastity. But, as with colonic irrigation, 'cleansing' masks an altogether uglier truth; that achieving purification can sometimes require brutal and dirty methods. When applied to human populations, the theoretical construct refers to expulsion, deportation, and detention. In practice it spells suffering and terror.

I was fully aware that cleansing does not necessarily apply only to 'ethnic' groups. In fact, its inclusion may have over-simplified a rather more complex situation where characteristics of religion, language and class were arguably just as much the determinants of division as ethnicity. Nevertheless, the words were carefully chosen, and their use was deliberate.

So, if I wasn't to focus on sectarian differences, should I instead focus on race? Croats were fond of deriding Serbs as 'Slavs' and Bosnians as 'Turks' or 'Gypsies' as if they were somehow inferior races. But was this dismissiveness based on race, or ethnicity? And anyway, what was the difference between the two?

Race, I was pretty sure, was largely a matter of biology, and referred to a person's physical characteristics, such as bone structure, type of hair, shape of eyes, and skin colour. Ethnicity, however, was a bit less tangible and more about sociology. It therefore referred to cultural factors, including nationality, language, and religion even though these could be ill-defined and were not mutually exclusive. More pertinent perhaps is that ethnicity connotes common cultural characteristics and a sense of shared group history.

From the Enlightenment onwards, scientists have group humanity into races and claimed that these have distinct characteristics. In her book superior, Angela Saini convincingly argues that this entire enterprise is bogus: people from different regions may differ in appearance, but this doesn't translate into consistent genetic attributes. 'Race,' she writes, 'is as biologically real as witches on broomsticks.' Rather than having anything to do with science, racial categorisation has long been thought of as being chiefly a means for white Westerners to bolster their sense of superiority—justifying the subjugation of other peoples in the process—by imbuing it with a veneer of scientific rationality.

But did history repeat itself in the Balkans? For, while race science was officially abandoned after the Second World War, it could be argued that it never really went away but was merely festering in the shadows. The resurgence of far-right populism after the collapse of communism and the rise of authoritarian leaders looking to add intellectual ballast to their prejudices, seemed to have made an alarming return with Milošević.

I couldn't tell Serbs and Croats apart just by looking at them, and, when speaking at least, they seemed to share a common language. They were both Christians too, even though one was Orthodox and the other Roman Catholic.

But the real difference between race and ethnicity is related to how we identify ourselves. A person does not choose his or her race; it is assigned by society based on physical features. Ethnicity, however, is a matter of choice, and involves self-identification through which language, social norms, customs, and cultures we assimilate. It is not just a matter of where you are born or which church your parents attend.

Overall then, and despite the fact that the two could be highly subjective, with lines between the two concepts being frequently blurred, it seemed fairly obvious to me that it was not sectarian or racial differences that lay at the heart of the current conflict, but ethnic.

More difficult was trying to work out whether this was a civil war based on sectarian division along the lines of Northern Ireland or Beirut.

As with race, I thought I knew a thing or two about sectarianism. I had, after all, been personally involved in trying to keep the peace between religious factions in both places.

But sectarianism is not just about religion. It is all about excessive devotion to any group or sect based on bigotry and discrimination which go on to fuel feelings of inferiority and superiority. These factions, groups, or sub-groups can be aligned as much by economics, class, or politics as by any religious affiliation, and their adherents often believe that for the achievement of their own political, religious, or social project, their opponents must either convert or be purged.

To a Brit, the term 'sectarian' usually refers to violent conflict along religious or political lines, for example between nationalists and unionists in Northern Ireland or between Shia and Sunni

Muslims in Iraq. The fact that such conflicts can be motivated by social inequity and criminality is largely forgotten. Non-sectarians believe that free association and tolerance of different political and religious beliefs are the cornerstone to pluralism and peace.

Sectarianism is a highly subjective and emotive word, as it reflects often violently-held opinions and perspectives over what is considered right and wrong. In the modern sense, it usually refers to religion.

To qualify as 'ethnic cleansing', the removal of a population designated by race, religion, language, or class must be deliberate, systematic, controlled, and forced. The intention must also be for it to be irreversible. It is, in other words, an essentially permanent political act of social engineering to which forethought and planning has been applied at the central level.

More pragmatically, the perpetrator could be any organisation that has the ability to exercise coercive power over specific territory. The most typical organisation that fulfils this criterion is obviously the state. However, from a conceptual perspective, if non-state actors such as militias or insurgent organisations acquire the ability to exercise coercive power over given territory, there are also capable of perpetrating ethnic cleansing. Indeed, the apparently ad-hoc nature of the practice in Vukovar in late 1991 by the notorious warlord Arkan and his White Eagles seems to be a case in point.

The second and most essential characteristic of 'ethnic cleansing' is that the intended target of violence is an ethnic group rather than individual members selected on some other criteria. This brings into question the definition of what constitutes an ethnic group. Ethnic groups are distinct from smaller units such as clans or kinship groups as, like nations, they are 'imagined communities' in the sense that their members will probably not know most of their fellow members, meet them, or even hear of them. In essence, Max Weber suggests that such a group of people either self-ascribe or are ascribed by others to a category defined by what he calls 'common descent'.

The third important characteristic of 'ethnic cleansing' is that it refers to cases in which populations are moved involuntarily and permanently from a specific territory. Perpetrators use a variety of methods including mass killings, terror, compulsory population exchange agreements, and deportations. In other words, 'ethnic cleansing' is any event in which an organisation that has the capability to use coercion and terror in a given territory in order to deport a substantial part of an ethnic group that lives within that territory.

But this didn't explain the motivation. The assumption in the case of Milošević and the Serb political leadership was that they had ideological goals and used 'ethnic cleansing' as a means of achieving these goals based on a causal logic which argued that early modern European states used violence against specific groups in order to engender a sense of collective identity in the rest of the population. But this does not explain or provide a convincing account of why the general population chose to believe leaders that depicted other ethnicities as dangerous or undesirable. After all, until the outbreak of hostilities Serbs and Croats had lived side-by-side either in the same village or in neighbouring villages, often worked together, and interacted on a daily basis.

Mulling over the emotional drivers underpinning this causal logic, it seemed that fear, revenge, resentment and prejudice were the most likely culprits, with resentment probably best describing the context of the time as it reflected the changing status and hierarchy between the different ethnic groups, including, for example, Croats suddenly being given limited access to political and administrative positions and overnight changes to school curricula which favoured one interpretation of the past over another.

It is not difficult to see resentment building in such circumstances.

As a practice, 'ethnic cleansing' is about creating a climate of fear that coerces people to 'voluntarily' flee their homes as a direct or indirect consequence of an actual or implied threat. It uses the tactics of terrorism and humiliation to bring this about. Certainly, to cause people to flee their homes in the dead of night in a blizzard—which is what I witnessed—the motivation must have been pretty drastic. Such motivations don't occur on the spur of the moment but accrue over time until some event occurs which spurs individuals, families or entire communities into action.

The builds slowly, insidiously, and without any hint of violence. People from the 'wrong' ethnic group, especially civil servants, begin to lose their jobs on the flimsiest of pretexts; they are harassed at checkpoints on the road, with minor faults found on their vehicles or irregularities in their paperwork necessitating them to report to police stations far away; access to health services becomes more difficult, with consultations cancelled with no warning and no reason given; their children come home from school crying having had nationalistic abuse shouted at them in the playground; a different language suddenly predominates in the curriculum; telephones get disconnected, and the repair man never seems to be available. Day-to-day harassment and minor infringements of civil liberty like this escalate to the point where street muggings increase in frequency with no apparent action taken by the police; verbal abuse becomes more vulgar; pregnant women are told they can no longer give birth in the local hospital; death threats drop through the letterbox; homes, shops and places of worship mysteriously catch fire or blow up, with the fire service taking hours to arrive; lists are published indicating each family's ethnic origin; and letters are received from the local authorities saying that the departure of one family member is conditional upon the departure of the entire family. Eventually, when the pressure has become unbearable, a single obscene act of violence — even the rumour of one — is enough to prompt whole villages to pack their bags and evacuate overnight but not before having been forced to sign documents stating that their property has been permanently abandoned and voluntarily made over to the aggressor. For a single act of violence to prompt such a drastic decision, it must be very obscene indeed and constitute terrorism rather than criminality. And they were.

The two methods most favoured in East Slavonia were beheadings, castration and gang rape, usually committed in front of the victim's parents, children or other family members. In one village, a grandmother was beheaded in front of her family and her head stuck on a pole at the end of the street. The village was assembled to witness the gruesome sight and told they had 24-hours to leave or the same fate would befall them. In another, a teenage girl was stripped naked, her breasts nailed to the kitchen table, after which she was vaginally and anally raped by over 20 men.

It was the same in the sullen city of Banja Luka in Northern Bosnia which was taken by general Ratko Mladic's Bosnian Serb forces in April 1992 almost without a shot being fired. As head of the new humanitarian aid office in the ECMM, I had gone there shortly afterwards to discuss possible aid convoy routes into northern Bosnia. I was there the night Serb paramilitaries started blowing up the city's Ottoman mosques. Cold and with only a nervous Italian driver for protection, I shivered under the bed sheets in the

Catholic Bishop's Palace—not a wise place for a supposedly neutral observer to stay, but the only bed available for the night—as the explosions boomed and echoed into the small hours. Under strict curfew, I was in no position to investigate what was going on. In any event, the noises seemed to me to be no worse than what had been going on in Vinkovci a few weeks earlier. By the time I was allowed to see for myself the result of this orgy of destruction, not only was the rubble being removed by mechanical diggers but pigs were wandering amidst the devastation, herded by smirking militiamen. This was the ultimate insult for a Muslim.

It was only then that I realised what the ethnic cleansing project was really all about. It was not just a military tactic but an explicit war aim; as much about methodically humiliating a people and destroying their culture as it was about killing them. The more terrified non-Serbs could be made to feel, the more likely they were not simply to flee but to not ever return. Of necessity, the process involved the re-writing of Yugoslavia's past and doing so in cyrillic script. Until then, ethnic cleansing had been limited in my mind to terror and forcible eviction; Serbs from Croatia—the Serbs might have perfected ethnic cleansing but the Croats had been guilty of it as well—and Croats from Serbia... including the three bits of Croatia with large Serb majorities. But now it was cultural identity that was being erased. Where mosques had once stood, the foundations for Orthodox churches were being laid. Not only that but settlers were being moved into well-kept apartments in the high-rise buildings around the city limits. Serbs who had fled their homes in Croatia during the early phases of the Serbo-Croat war in the Autumn of 1991 were being resettled into properties that, until only weeks before, had belonged to Muslim and Croat families who had lived in the region for generations and who had themselves been expelled. The transformation of public spaces was equally radical. Libraries, statues and theatres were transformed overnight into building sites where foundations were laid for alternative structures whose erection was as essential a measure of their victory as the murder and dispersal of the non-Serb population.

In Slavonia, and later in Bosnia, people's livelihoods went first. Non-Serbs were quietly excluded from all senior positions which they might be called upon to make what the new authorities described as 'independent decisions'. In practice, this meant that company directors and senior management were either dismissed or demoted to the most menial positions in their companies. Even medical professionals, whose skills were desperately needed, were dismissed. In a series of non-violent steps, the Serb authorities single-mindedly eliminated the middle-class future of the Muslim and Croat populations until the was nothing left but hopelessness and despair. The firing itself was only the beginning. Once someone's dismissal had been made known officially the next step was for a letter to be sent demanding that the person vacate the apartment in which he or she had been living. Thus, to be deprived of a job was to stop being a citizen, to be forcibly moved from the status of non-Serb to the status of non-person in a matter of hours.

The war that Mladic waged in Croatia, the goal of which was to carve an ethnically pure Serb territory out of the carcass of the Croatian state, succeeded in its aims almost completely. By the time a UN-brokered ceasefire had been arranged—the one I was supposed to be monitoring—he had what he wanted. By the late spring of 1992, as the apple and cherry blossom bloomed across the verdant hills of Bosnia he also had the model for the pogrom that was steadily seeping across the entire country. This was not war as I knew it, even civil war. It was the process the Serbs had undertaken to consolidate their victory. Once again, with the siege of Sarajevo having only just begun, I was probably the first foreigner to witness the next hideous phase of the 'ethnic cleansing' project that was to culminate in Srebrenica over three years later.

'Ethnic cleansing'—or some variant of it—has been going on for over 3,000 years, possibly longer. Although its fundamental drivers have changed significantly over the centuries, this barbaric practice has always been directed at minority groups considered subversive and therefore potentially dangerous. First it was religion, then it was idealism, and now ethnicity. Why the change?

The answer lies in different interpretations of collective identity. Social groups that define themselves in religious terms cleanse religious minorities; those that see themselves in terms of class, get rid of class enemies, and so on. For their survival, much depends on whether these identities are natural or synthetic, genetically determined or politically inspired.

Either way, representative democracy gives resentment, real or imagined, a voice. Because it tilts individual rights at the expense of group rights in a system in which one person equals one vote, numerical strength translates into political power. If the society is multi-ethnic—especially if it is ethnically stratified—the larger ethnic group usually prevails. And if minority rights are not sufficiently protected, minorities are forced to submit to decisions unfavourable to their interests.

Representative democracy would not be quite so lethal—from the ethnic point of view at least—without the creation of the nation state, a concept which coalesces the ideals of freedom and self-determination into the combustible mixture we now call 'nationalism.'

Until that point, I thought I knew what a 'country' was. As Hobsbawm alludes, it is either yours or somewhere else; somewhere other; somewhere forever foreign, where language, culture, religion and custom are different. But, in truth, the concept is notoriously hazy. Countries are not nearly as stable as you might think. Countries come and countries go. Just a few years before, the disintegration of the Soviet Union spawned no fewer than 15 new states. Here was the breakup of former-Yugoslavia about to spawn five-and-a-half more (if you include Kosovo).

So, surrounded by newly printed Croatian national flags fluttering from every house, I was forced into thinking about what exactly defines a country? And is it the same thing as a nation, or a state? The concept of nationhood might seem clear enough, but as soon as you try to find a clearer definition you quickly run up against a series of discrepancies, exceptions and anomalies. An apparently straightforward answer might be that all 'real' countries have a seat at the General Assembly of the United Nations, the world's most important state-based international organisation. But where does that leave Palestine or The Holy See who don't? And what about Crimea and Tibet?

Then there are countries that only have UN membership when considered as a group. The United Kingdom of Great Britain and Northern Ireland—to give the UK its full title—is one of these. The four separate countries of England, Wales, Scotland and Northern Ireland are united under a single parliament through a series of legally binding Acts of Union. So, when it comes to international relations, these four countries are represented by the UK government. But Wales is a principality, while Scotland—a country not so much seeking to secede but reassert its national sovereignty—is a nation. They are different. That's why one has a national assembly while the other has a parliament. Both models provide a measure of autonomy, but neither are independent.

Furthermore, Scotland has its own legal and educational systems, and can print its own currency.

And it gets trickier. All four countries enter football teams into the World Cup, but only Great Britain is represented at the Olympics. And Great Britain, being made up only of Scotland, Wales and England, is not the same thing as the United Kingdom. And where does that leave the Channel Islands? Or the Isle of Man? The Isle of Man lies in the Irish Sea roughly midway between the four countries of the United Kingdom. Yet, while it is a self-governing dependency of the British Crown and the British monarch is head of state, the island is not a 'British Isle' as most British people know it. Their first language is Manx rather than English, and they make their own rules. Their parliament, the Tynwald, is the world's oldest continuous ruling body and has governed the island since the arrival of the Vikings in the late eighth century.

While the notion of fixed territory was fluctuating around me, there is no question that our concept of nationhood remains central to our sense of identity. Where we were born still dominates who we think we are. Much as some of us might like to think of ourselves as 'international nomads', rather than citizens of any one nation state, we won't get very far without a passport issued by a national government. As Professor Nick Middleton put it in his book *An Atlas of Countries That Don't Exist,* 'National territory still has an enduring allure.' And nation states work hard to keep it that way, defending borders, protecting citizens, and strengthening national cohesion through, for example, flying flags and embedding patriotic images in the nation's currency.

However, depiction of national borders on the world map portrays only a selected version of reality. Many recognised countries have borders that have never been precisely defined and agreed by treaty through a process known as 'delimitation. And a large number of those that have been delimited have never been demarcated i.e actually marked out on the ground. The Durand line demarcates the border between Afghanistan and Pakistan with a series of white painted cairns put there by the British in the late 19th century. On the other side of Pakistan, however, the lack of delimitation and demarcation frequently spirals into disputes between it and its Indian neighbour, who, as the latest sabre-rattling involving the downing of each other's fighter-jets made clear as recently as March 2019, have disagreed for more than 60 years over which parts of Jammu & Kashmir belongs to whom. These and other borders have been drawn in atlases with what appears to be a definitive line, many of them straight, but in reality many of these boundaries are far from conclusive.

The word 'nation' is reserved for a social, ethnic or cultural group that may or may not have its own country i.e territory bounded by defined borders. Native American Navajo 'indians' are recognised as a nation within the United States of America. But, not having territory, they are not considered a 'state'.

A widely accepted legal definition of a 'state' was hammered out at a meeting in Uruguay in the 1930s, where article 1 of the Montevideo Convention sets out the four essential criteria for statehood: a permanent population; a defined territory; a government; and the capacity to enter into relations with other states. The German social and political scientist Max Weber defined statehood in rather blunter terms: as 'a monopoly of the legitimate use of violence over a given territory.' Certainly, organised violence has helped many countries gain and hold territory and continues to be a potent symbol of national strength. Whatever definition you prefer, countries display at least the outward trappings of national consciousness, including a flag, some form of identifiable government which offers protection, a claim to territory, as well as a seriousness of purpose. But the fact that there is no one, universally acknowledged definition means that their interest is, to some extent, inherently arbitrary. And just the night before I had been standing on the edge of a minefield well inside what, until then, the world had recognised as Croatia only to find that someone else had a different idea of where the border post should be.

Inevitably, my thoughts would turn to the idea of identity when faced with such realities on the ground. Who do any of us think we are? Gender, religion, race, nationality, class, and culture give contours to our sense of self; they shape our view of the world and the world's view of us. Yet, like the war-damaged buildings all around me, the collective and complex identities they spawn are riddled with contradictions and pock-marked with falsehoods. It took a while for me to get to know the myths underpinning Croatia's collective identity, myths that others were not just blind to, but contemptuously dismissive of. During my few short weeks in Croatia my assumptions about how identity works had not just been challenged but upended.

It quickly became apparent that in the Balkans one's sense of self was forged by a childhood full of distortions and half-truths, of stories of conflicts lost and won, many of which had happened centuries before. And, as always, it is the half-truths that blind us. And it wasn't just the false history. Religion was more about ideology than conviction or belief. Long-discredited notions of race were alive and well in the Balkans. And the cherished concept of the sovereign nation—particularly its right to self-determination—rather than being incoherent and unstable was almost a divine right. Tito's brand of communism had entrenched class systems rather than reformed them. And the idea of Western capitalism as a shining beacon, not the grubby, winner-take-all shimmering mirage it really is, was everything.

The tragedy lay in their individual and collective inability to realise that their true place in a fast-changing post-communist European order was the result of mistaken identity. And this was true of Serb, Croat, and Bosnian alike. And it was this that fuelled some of the worst atrocities that were now unfolding around us and which were set to get worse in the years to come.

A sense of identity works at two fundamental levels: while being something which defines the individual as themselves, it simultaneously refers to something that people share. For most of history it has been the sameness that has mattered, and identity tended to be a group designation. Clans, ethnicities, linguistic groups, and religions went to great lengths to distinguish themselves from others.

An individual's identity involves three fundamental elements: the first concerns the self, the person looking at you in the mirror. The second is that an individual's identity is contingent not on one's own self-image but on the recognition of others, some of whom you may not have met. And the third is the isolation that follows when that recognition is not forthcoming, or is subverted.

Self-image is largely a personal matter, beyond external control. When you put the other two elements together, however, you quickly see why the provision and policing of identity became one of the foundations of the modern nation state, and the lives within it. Identity is about control.

A person's sense of who they are depends on many things, all of which are not necessarily either stable or singular. People identify themselves in many ways, often simultaneously. For myself, I count myself lucky to be being part of a Scottish clan, the Murray's. But I talk with an English accent and count myself as British. Later in life, when working with the European Commission, I began to identify more as European.

All of which holds little weight without documentary evidence in areas regulated by the state: finance, housing, land ownership, employment, marital status etc. and it is only the state that has the power to issue a legal identity. As with the authority to issue fiat money, assignment identity has become a state monopoly. When states abuse this power, individuals suffer. Identity, like cash, can be taken away at any time by the state that issues it. This gives them power not just to identify and legitimise their people, but to organise their lives.

In times of economic stress and cultural anxiety people resort to anchoring themselves in their sense of place, tradition, and tribe. Insecurity makes you reach for these identities as a means of imparting meaning, as a sort of protection, and eventually a defining part of who you are. This sense of belonging, of who 'we' are, is very tenacious and is nowhere more durable than in what the political scientist Benedict Anderson called 'The imagined community of the nation.'

There didn't appear to be much that was 'imagined' by the Croats that surrounded me about the Croatian nation; the idea seemed very real to them, as real as it must have seemed to the Anglo-Saxons in 6th Century Britain where the concept of the 'nation state' was born.

The British tend to think of the Norman Conquest in 1066 as the turning point in the history of their country. But the Saxon conquest some 500 years earlier was even more seminal since it created both the reality and the idea of

England as an autonomous nation state. Looking back, it is scarcely possible to exaggerate the scale of the Saxon incursions from what is now northern Germany. Up to 200,000 people flooded into a native population which by then had been reduced by raids, famine and disease to less than 2 million. Proportionately, it was the largest immigration that the British Isles had ever known. Moreover, as most of the incomers were men, it quickly turned from immigration into conquest. DNA evidence shows that up to 90% of the native male population was displaced—either killed or driven West—and their women, their villages and their farms taken over by the incomers. These events, outlined in the Anglo-Saxon Chronicles, are among the earliest written records in Europe of ethnic cleansing at its most savagely effective.

This period marks the annihilation of everything that was Roman about Britain: the law, the language, the literature, the religion, and the politics all vanished to be replaced with a new language, new gods and a new, very different, set of political and social values. And from these, in time, a nation would be created and eventually an empire to rival Rome. English was to replace Latin as the *lingua franca;* English common law would challenge Roman law as the dominant legal system; and they would devise, in free-market economics, a new form of business that would transform human wealth and welfare. Most importantly perhaps, they would invent a new form of politics which depended on participation and consent rather than on the top-down autocracy of Rome.

All this made the physical barriers between Hibernia—now known as Scotland—and Wales redundant. Both Hadrian's Wall, which stretched from coast to coast across n orthern Britain and Offa's Dyke which stretched north-south along the entirety of the Welsh border fell into disrepair.

An idea of England had been forged that was more than simply cultural and linguistic, it was political as well. Or, rather uniquely for Europe at the time, it was a combination of all three. In other words, what the Vikings called *Ængla Land* had become an Anglo-Saxon nation state in which the rulers and the ruled spoke the same language. In 1066 this all stopped, and for the next four centuries England was administered in Latin and governed in French. Anglo-Saxon, instead, became the patois of the poor and dispossessed.

But what of the ideas and institutions of the Anglo-Saxon state, with its notions of consensual politics, of participatory government, and with a monarchy that was in some sense responsible for, and accountable to, the people? Would they vanish? Or adapt to live another day? Croatia, too, had its royal dynasties and its feudal Župans. No chance was lost to mention this to any inquisitive foreigner. So, was it to resurrect such an idea some thirteen hundred years later?

But what of tribalism? Since tiptoeing gingerly through those Croatian minefields, I had sometimes wondered what it must be like to live in a truly tribal society. Living among Serbs and Croats and later with Rwandan Hutu's and Tutsi', you get curious about how the collective mind can come so undone. What's it like to see the contours of someone's face, or hear an accent, or learn where someone's from, and almost reflexively know that they are 'other' and that they're not on your side? How do you live peacefully for years among fellow countrymen and then find yourself suddenly engaged in the mass murder of humans who look like you, live like you, even pray like you, but in whom tiny quirks of the past mean they must be killed or forced out before they kill or force you out? In the Balkans, a long period of relative peace imposed by communism was being shattered in front of my eyes by a form of brutal tribal warfare that no outsider could possibly understand as previously intermingled citizens split into irreconcilable groups.

I had seen tribal loyalties turn Beirut, Lebanon's beautiful, cosmopolitan capital, into an urban wasteland in 1983, and, as a 'neutral' peacekeeper, had been shot at for daring to try to stem the carnage. I left the Balkans once the Bosnian war came to its exhausted, grudging close and went to Burundi and then Rwanda to learn what nearly one million people buried in shallow mass graves smells like. I was among the first to witness Serb tanks smashing into Albanian villages in Kosovo and was expelled from Sudan for confronting the government in Khartoum with the evidence of what they were doing to their own people in Darfur. I have lived in Bangladesh and seen how miserable life can be for refugees from neighbouring countries.

We have been hardwired by evolution into craving a sense of belonging, to be accepted as part of a group, a tribe if you like. Somewhere along the line this group survival instinct got swept up by the drug of community and we became seduced by the idea that 'we', our group, are 'right and good' while 'they', the other group, are 'wrong and evil.' This very human—and very misguided—mentality has led to a whole host of disastrous social and political consequences for time immemorial.

Tribalism is not about family. Nor is it about clan or kinship. It is about attitudes and behaviours that stem from loyalty to the dogma of a much larger social construction.

Racism and all the other ugly '-isms' grow from a primitive, inchoate force lurking deep within us all, a force called 'tribalism' where we are instinctively hostile to those of another race, religion, nationality, or class. However hard we try to suppress it, this force compels us to become angry, bitter, jealous, and ultimately resentful towards everything outside of the tribe. However hard we try to rationalise our baser instincts, we realise that the drivers can be as much about politics as about ethnicity, or as much about economics as about language.

This 'Us versus Them' mentality has not led us anywhere productive or appealing. It only leads down a path of suffering and destruction which everybody says they don't want but at the same time do nothing to prevent.

Tribalism is not just one aspect of human experience; it's the default human experience.

It comes more naturally to us than any other way of life. For the overwhelming majority of our time on this planet, the tribe was the only form of human society. We lived for tens of thousands of years in compact, largely egalitarian groups of around 50–100 people, connected to each other by genetics and language, mostly not in writing. Most tribes occupied their own familiar territory, with widespread sharing of food and no private property.

Cohesion was essential to survival, and our first religions emerged for precisely this purpose. As Dominic Johnson argues in his recent book *God Is Watching You*, almost all indigenous societies had a common concept of the supernatural, and almost all of them saw their worst threats—hunger, disease, natural disasters, a loss in battle—as a consequence of disobeying a God. Religion therefore fused with communal identity and purpose, it was integral to keeping the enterprise afloat, and the idea of people within a tribe believing in different Gods was incomprehensible.

The tribes that best survived—and thereby transmitted their genes to us—were, moreover, those most acutely aware of outsiders and potential foes. A failure to notice incoming strangers could end your life in an instant, and an indifference to the appearances of other human beings could mean defeat at the hands of rivals or the collapse of a tribe altogether. And so we became a deeply cooperative species — but primarily with our own kind. The notion of living alongside people who do not look like us and treating them as our fellows was meaningless for most of human history.

The nation state did not abolish this feeling; instead they co-opted it by forming a mega-tribe that united people around shared national rituals, a sense of collective defence, symbols, music, history, mythology, and events. It is the core unit of belonging that makes a national body politic possible.

Healthy tribalism endures in civil society in benign and overlapping ways. We find a sense of belonging and an unconditional pride in our neighbourhood and community and in our ethnic and social identities and their rituals. You need look no further than any sports fan and the intense 'tribal' loyalties that being a fan inculcates. Football (soccer) in Europe provides perhaps the most glaring example of where fandom can lead if tribal passions and loyalties are threatened.

It is this sense of belonging and loss that, when manipulated, shapes the destinies of nations. A political discourse rooted in a sense of difference, a sense of cultural superiority, ensures that patriotism, which doesn't require an enemy, morphs into nationalism, which always does. And nationalism is easily forged by a political blacksmith wielding the hammer of competing narratives on the anvil of a shared myth.

Patriotism is one thing, nationalism quite another. Patriotism, I had always thought, is about tolerance and reason. It is a love of country, of place, of culture. Nationalism, on the other hand, is a hatred of everybody else's. At least, General de

Gaulle's infamous epithet was one of the lessons I had absorbed while an officer cadet at Sandhurst.

Like religion, nationalism is capable of bringing out the best in people as well as the worst. That much was already clear. It can inspire them to live and work together in pursuit of a common goal, even the common good. But here it was filling everyone I met with a terrifying, righteous certainty which seemed to be spiralling into ever-more contempt for 'other'. I had come across bigotry on a daily basis in Northern Ireland, with Catholics spitting on Protestants—and vice versa—at any opportunity. I had even had to deal with what happens once spitting turns to shooting and bombing. And it's not pretty. It wasn't pretty here either. Far from it.

It was either all about 'the nation', or it wasn't. Yugoslavia was, like so many federations, something of a false construct, glued together in the wake of the Second World War by the idealistic bonds of communism and little else. Slovenia, Croatia, Serbia, Montenegro, Macedonia, and, to an extent, Bosnia and Hercegovina had existed long before Yugoslavia came about. Like most other nations, they had existed for centuries.

Once it had been grasped by a stunned Europe in the early 19th century that the divine rule of emperors and kings was coming to an end, the concept of nationhood began to gain legitimacy. The concept was built on three philosophical pillars:

Legitimacy is derived from the people, and is not handed down from above. Philosophers like

Rousseau and Locke drew on a well-established sense of national cause to explain how individual citizens have the right to join freely in a nation whose sole purpose is to protect and benefit them. Authority stems directly from the nation, they said.

Government is not just an agreement between individuals, but also a statement of the general will. Yes, the individual can have rights, but so can the collective. Britain's Magna Carta was an early example of this. Sadly, however, governments have used and abused the principal ever since.

But one person's patriotic pride is another's nationalistic prejudice. The belief that nationalism would fade away in the communist utopia of post-war Yugoslavia, was always naïve. The only question was what form it would take.

There is always a central fiction that underpins the story, that provides the foundational myth around which centuries of half-truth swirl. In the United States, for example, Americans see themselves as inheriting a 'land of the free' and 'home of the brave' but subscribe to a constitution which embraces slavery. In this sense, we are what we forget, a sentiment reflected by the French philosopher Ernest Renan who said, 'Nations are held together as much by what they forget as what they remember.' The essential characteristic of a nation, in other words, is that its people must have many things in common, including their common ability to forget.

Like the Czech-born novelist Milan Kundera, he saw the struggle of man against power as the struggle of memory against forgetting. History, such people argue, is not just a matter of the victor writing the story but how they go on to ensure that memory is expunged. These are, after all, two sides of the same coin.

In this sense, the full history of the 1991–1995 war of Yugoslav secession has yet to be written. Meanwhile, across the former conflict zones of Croatia, Serbia, Bosnia and Kosovo, whole peoples seem to have been afflicted by a kind of historical amnesia. As in Putinist Russia, where it is easier to believe in a glorious Soviet past than to accept that the twin totalitarian evils of Nazism and Stalinism were but mirror images of each other, Serbs, Croats, Bosnians and Albanians piece together their future in a state of wilful denial, their biases combining with the human brain's heuristic ability to forget the bad bits to concoct yet another chapter in the ongoing saga of the Balkans.

Believing in the collective power of these shared fictions is fundamental to realising a sense of national identity, and that it is, as ethicist Kwame Anthony Appiah has since pointed out, 'the lies that bind us' to a sense of something greater than ourselves.

Like the English parish with its Norman church spire nestling in a green and pleasant oaky vale, the Balkan Vilayet is a miniature welfare state, responsible for its poor. It's important to know to which you belong as your welfare, indeed your survival, was tied to a very practical sense of belonging. You had to keep outsiders out or your fragile social safety net and its very limited resources would be threatened. Local rivalries grow from this sense of localised belonging. You can see an extreme expression of this every year during the *Palio* horse-races in Siena, Italy where different wards (contrade) of the city loudly and proudly parade their colours. People find it difficult to adapt to changing cultural expectations when their belief system says they belong to a local place.

Former Yugoslavia wasn't suffering from a surfeit of pluralism at the time, far from it; the various states that had made up this uneasy alliance for over thirty years were emerging, blinking into the harsh realities of a post-communist dawn. The sense of insecurity was palpable and it was clear for anybody with eyes to see that there was everything to play for. It is into such uncertain and volatile environments that bullies find it all too easy to play power politics. Government of, by, and for the people is far from uppermost in the minds of such people who will instead use the media to claim that shadowy enemies abroad are subverting the state, undermining the national culture, or insulting the majority religion. As so often before and since, this was just a pretext to purge the judiciary, muzzle the press, and put friends and relations in charge of supposedly independent institutions.

The nationalist rhetoric of Milosević and Tuđman allowed no room for their neighbouring states to become networked. Their policy was that each could become a fortress where immigration and multiculturalism was to be prevented from entering the walls of Mokrice Castle in Slovenia and Zagreb's *Gorni Grad* (old town) at all costs. History shows that all attempts to divide the world into clear-cut nations have resulted in war. Knowing this, society was told to raise the drawbridge and man the walls, telling their neighbours to go and screw themselves in the process.

The sadness is that no one seemed to realise that establishing a new identity does not mean having to abolish all cultural, religious and national differences. As a Scot living in England before serving in Northern Ireland with a Welsh regiment, I knew I was no different to any Serb or any Croat. I could be loyal to one and, at the same time, several identities, my family, my clan, my regiment, my country. I was even proud of working for a European Union bent on preserving peace in its own backyard; the reason it had been established in the first place.

This is not to say that sometimes different loyalties might not collide. Sometimes family came before work, or the regiment before the family, and juggling the different priorities made it not always easy to decide what to do. But in each case one had to balance the conflicting demands of self-interest and the greater good. At no point did patriotism allow nationalistic sentiments to become an impossible barrier to the creation of my own identity. It's not that I didn't think about it, I did. Lurking around half frozen in the wintry bushes of Northern Ireland in order to protect some Protestant landowner from his catholic cousins, or vice versa, gave one plenty of opportunity to do so. I had seen bigotry up close and personal but subsumed my personal feelings for the greater good it was my duty to protect.

But that was years before. I had been an advertising executive for six years since then, and more recently, an aid worker. Now, here I was, a political analyst working from my country's Foreign Ministry as a 'humanitarian adviser' observing up close and personal the workings of someone else's. Human identities are quite adaptable. National ones, it appeared, rather less so.

But what was it that made all sides think that this conflict was worth waging in the first place? Political rhetoric alone is not usually enough to turn decent, law-abiding folk into mass murderers. Yes, Tuđman and Milošević were opportunistic, callous villains but that does not mean that everyone else, whether soldier or civilian, was a victim. There must have been something deeper lurking inside the psyche of the Yugoslav soul, a flammable spirit, a yearning resentment perhaps, waiting to be ignited.

Certainly, Milošević's early speeches over *Kosovo Polje* were riddled with an existential angst which spoke to the nationalist cause, and which employed the philosophical tenets of Nietzsche to challenge his listeners to become what they could be. His words did not fall on stony ground, mostly because somewhere in the misty bogs of Serbian mythology tendrils of self-doubt and victimhood were always swirling. The internal self can easily be warped by the external context in such a febrile atmosphere where the wily alchemy of power and influence slips unseen into human consciousness almost without anyone noticing, there to begin the deconstruction of fact and reconstruction of myth. In this sense, the rhetoric of nationalism merely allowed what was already present in the listener's heart and mind to blossom. Or did this process of mental re-engineering polarise and entrench the worst aspects of themselves, making people behave in ways they otherwise would not have done?

The conflict was effectively a civil war, with Serbs and Croats—later Bosnian Serbs and Bosnian Croats—convinced of their manifest destinies, and fighting for land, assets, and ethnic purity. These were hardly lofty ideals or valid reasons to kill your cousin. But kill they did, and in large numbers, frequently without discrimination.

The underlying causes of conflict are always more complicated than this, and the former-Yugoslavia is no exception. As Michael Mann put it in his book *The Dark Side of Democracy*, 'Culture is vague and descent usually fictitious.' The last battle ever fought on British soil took place in 1745 not far from my home in Scotland at Culloden, and was about the Catholic and Protestant religions just as much as it was about rights of succession or nationhood. Most of the Highland clansmen on Bonnie Prince Charlie's side spoke English as well as Gaelic, and more Scots fought on the English side than on the Scottish. This is what is meant by culture being vague, and is no less part of the fiction than that experienced by a Croat soldier with a Serb mother fighting to defend Vukovar.

No, what really identifies one ethnic group over another is the extent to which its political history is shared. Yes, language and religion are important, but they're not as definitive as they had initially appeared to me to be. Serbo-Croat sounded the same when spoken but was unintelligible when written down as the Croats used Latin script whereas the Serbs used Cyrillic.

When moving to another country it takes a while to adjust to the currents and rhythms of daily life. When that country is on a war footing, everybody is readjusting. For me, the trolley-buses were a novelty as were the shops stocking rows and rows of what appeared to be little more than boiled cabbage. That nightclubs had two check-ins, one for coats, the other for guns, was also a novelty, and not just to me. But the biggest culture shock is always language which ebbs and flows around you like a river, confusing and unfathomable until you pick up a few commonly used phrases. Unlike Italian or Spanish, Serbo-Croat was not an easy language to decipher, but just because the words were new or even that most of them seem to have no vowels, but because they were spoken in staccato bursts at what I thought was excessive volume to the point that it sounded like everybody was arguing all the time rather than conversing.

Suddenly, here I was confronted once again with history. Not the remote, schoolboy history of the classroom, but the real living history of blood and myth, religion and redemption. Most people don't have cause to challenge their own history. They are happy with their place in its continuum and are only forced to ponder its relevance sporadically when travelling abroad or watching some dreadful event unfold on their TV screen.

I had come up close and personal with history before, however, first in Northern Ireland, and then in Beirut. In both cases, I had cause to question who was right, who was wrong, and what was any of this to do with me. Being neutral and impartial in such circumstances does not come easy, especially when your military role obliges you to be a tool of state politics. It doesn't take long to realise that there is no truth, no right and wrong, and here I was being reminded of this basic principle once again. Only, this time, I didn't have a gun in my hands. I was an outsider looking in, powerless and without influence. I wasn't part of it. I was just an observer.

But I was sceptical enough to know the observer is always somehow implicated and cannot be separated from the larger proceeding. I was familiar with the paradox of Schrödinger's cat and Walter Benjamin's essays on history. I knew Benjamin's theories that 'The state of emergency in which we live is not the exception but the rule,' and that 'There is no document of civilization which is not at the same time a document of barbarism.' I also knew from painful readings of Caesar's Punic Wars in Latin at school that history is written by the victor.

From a historical perspective, 'ethnic cleansing' seems to have happened in three distinct phases: In ancient times it was deployed as a political tool by which to control recently conquered foreign populations and as a source of slaves; during the Middle Ages it acquired a mostly religious character; and in the early modern period it took on the ethnic orientation we are familiar with today.

Sometime between the fourth and sixth centuries, the focal point of collective identity in Europe and the Middle East shifted to religion, and the change in patterns of 'ethnic' partition reflected this shift: it was now re-directed against religious minorities. Other forms of cleansing, including ethnic, did not entirely disappear, the elimination of Danes in England being a case in point. The tendency to define collective identity by religion probably reached its high point in the religious wars between Catholics and Protestants after the Reformation. But the major frontlines of this time pitted Christians against Muslims, with the northern boundary more or less running East-West along the Sava river.

In his seminal work on ethnic cleansing, Andrew Bell-Fialkoff describes this evolution as follows: 'But this change did not simply involve the shedding of the old religious identity and the acquisition of a new ethnic one, like the shedding of a snake's skin. Rather, the new national/ethnic identity was superimposed on the old one, adding a concentric circle to the old religious core. With the development of nationalism, however, it acquired a new significance and a new importance.'

BACK TO THE FUTURE

THE SECESSIONIST WARS that took place across former-Yugoslavia from Slovenia in 1991 to Kosovo ten years later show how easy it is to weaponise history and murder tens of thousands for the simple 'crime' of belonging to the 'wrong' ethnic group.

More recently, Richard Falk, the United Nations Special Rapporteur on Human Rights in the Occupied Palestinian Territories, told a news conference in 2014 that Israeli policies at the time 'bore unacceptable characteristics of colonialism, apartheid and ethnic cleansing.'

He was speaking against a backdrop of deadlocked peace talks and accelerating Israeli settlement expansion in the occupied West Bank and East Jerusalem which Palestinians say is dimming their hope of establishing a viable state on contiguous territory. Asked about his accusation of ethnic cleansing, Falk said that more than 11,000 Palestinians had lost their right to live in Jerusalem since 1996 due to Israel imposing residency laws favouring Jews and revoking Palestinian residence permits. 'The 11,000 is just the tip of the iceberg because many more are faced with possible challenges to their residency rights.' This compounded the 'ordeal of this extended, prolonged occupation', according to Falk, also an expert in international law and professor emeritus at Princeton University in the United States.

Falk added that, in his professional determination, Israeli policies in the West Bank appeared to amount to 'apartheid and segregation' with a de facto annexation of parts of the territory, denying the Palestinian right to self-determination.

Arriving in Zagreb, Croatia's capital in January 1992 and leaving after the fall of Knin in the Summer of 1995, I watched the Bosnian war unfold. From beginning to end, I witnessed with my own eyes the conscious manipulation of popular sentiment and how the deliberate use of myth and memory can subvert the truth and in its place instil distrust, fear, and ultimately hatred.

The murder of over 8,000 Muslim men and boys at Srebrenica in 1995 and the reverse ethnic cleansing of Knin a few months later were the final destinations in a journey that began with mere words.

Dünya and her fellow interpreters had grown up during a time when one national myth was being replaced by another. The old Yugoslavia that was swept away in the early 1990's had been founded during the Second World War when the struggle against fascism was shared by all ethnic groups. Its national moto was 'Brotherhood and Unity'. This was a story to unite all those who lived in the Federal Republic of Yugoslavia, Serb, Croat and Bosniak alike.

The communist wartime leader, Josip Tito died in 1980 and, in the decade that followed, the story of a peaceful, multi-ethnic state at ease with itself began to give way to something else.

The shift was subtle and insidious. Slowly but surely, as the decade proceeded, a quasi-religious millennial liberation narrative came to fore which positioned Serbs as a persecuted group going back to the Ottoman period; a group which had, in their telling, heroically defended Christendom against the rise of the Turk, and which had managed to preserve their language, history and religion over many centuries of Ottoman despotism.

By the end of the decade, every communist regime in Europe except that in Serbia had been toppled by populist uprisings. In Serbia, Milošević alone held on to power. He cemented that power by applying a potent mix of history, political theatre and ritual. In June 1989, as this series of democratic revolutions approached their zenith and the Berlin wall was about to fall, Milošević addressed a huge rally of fellow Serbs at Gaziemestan in their heartland of Kosovo. The occasion was the 600th anniversary of the infamous Battle of Kosovo Polje in 1389, the battle at which the medieval Serbian kingdom was defeated by an Ottoman army, ushering in centuries of Ottoman occupation across Serbia. Over the roar of tens of thousands of his fellow Serbs, he said that here they were once again, six hundred years later, once again engaged in an existential battle against a similar threat. The story resonated powerfully across Serbia and in those parts of Bosnia inhabited by ethnic Serbs who felt especially vulnerable. In hindsight, this speech demonstrated the beginnings of the process by which long-dormant ethnic enmity could be stoked.

Tensions of the past re-surface to challenge identity. Working with history, or representations of history often only loosely connected with reality, is a critical tool of identity politics. Collective hate is a product of organisation and mobilisation of groups. Milošević and later, the Bosnian Serb leader Radovan Karadic, argued that Serbs were once again facing the threat of extermination and that they had a duty to take up the heroic struggle for national unity and self-determination that had begun six centuries earlier. The message was clear: If you want to resist occupation and persecution you must be the one to initiate violence. Violence, said Karadic, is a unifying right and providence called for a 'necessary baptism by blood.'

As in Rwanda a few years later, religion was not left out. The Serbs would prevail, he said, because they are defined by their orthodox Christian faith. The Serbs had saved medieval Christian Europe from the Ottoman Turks. Any war would be a holy war. Liberation thus becomes intertwined with religion. It didn't take much imagination to see Muslims reconceptualised as Turks; not as neighbours and the fellow citizens they had been for hundreds of years but the living embodiment of Ottoman oppression.

It was very obvious to any outside observer with eyes to see in early 1992 that a shift in popular sentiment was accelerating and that long-held conceptions of 'who we are' no longer matched 'who we might become.' Propaganda was seeping in to contaminate the groundwater of public perception. Teachers, Doctors and Civil Servants began to ask ever-more personal questions about parentage, ethnicity, social class, and worship. Slowly but surely they too were becoming 'middle managers of ethnic cleansing' and began to turn rhetoric into a real and local reality.

The project of 'ethnic cleansing' was pursued systematically municipality by municipality. Although not so obvious in its earlier guises, the strategy was centrally directed. It was a top-down, state-sponsored project. Many of those who, wittingly or unwittingly took part said later that they should have seen the signs, and had they done so, they would have taken action to stop matters from spiralling out of control. Nazi prison camp guards said much the same. I was there. I saw what was going on. And, if it was obvious to me, it must have been doubly so to them.

The genocide as represented by the massacres at Srebrenica marked an escalation from the strategy of 'ethnic cleansing' that predated it. The change of gear forced the hand of an anguished world.

Tragically—and perhaps inevitably—the legacy endures. The Serbian struggle of the 1990's remains a central part of an emerging heroic narrative of the global far right today. The poetry and music of that struggle inspires groups like Islamic State and was even playing in the car of the man who murdered over fifty people, including women and children, in cold blood in Christchurch, New Zealand in March 2019 as he drove to the scene. This is the soundtrack of hate and 'ethnic cleansing'. The manifestos of hate have migrated from the killing fields of Croatia to the internet forums of the far-right. As 9/11 made starkly clear, it turns out that ancient enmities are not so ancient after all and we are not as immune as we like to think.

EPILOGUE

THIS ARTICLE BY SHAUN WALKERS was published in July 2020 on the 25th anniversary of the Srebrenica massacre and is reproduced verbatim with the permission of The Guardian Newspaper Group[28]. It is a bleak summary of what this book is about: How genocide, war crimes and ethnic cleansing are not the same in either intent or action; how selective is our memory; and how close we all are to barbarity.

---

28. https://www.theguardian.com/world/2020/jul/10/genocide-denial-gains-ground-25-years-after-srebrenica-massacre

GENOCIDE DENIAL GAINS GROUND 25 YEARS AFTER SREBRENICA MASSACRE

At the genocide memorial centre outside Srebrenica, thousands of simple white gravestones stretch across the gently inclined hillside for as far as the eye can see.

Nearby, over a number of days in July 1995, Bosnian Serb forces systematically murdered around 8,000 Bosniak (Bosnian Muslim) men and boys. It was the worst crime of the Bosnian war, and remains the only massacre on European soil since the second world war to be ruled a genocide.

Even today, remains of victims are still being found and identified. Owing to a cover-up operation to hide the crimes by digging up and dispersing the contents of mass graves, there are cases in which partial remains of the same individual have been found at as many as five sites several miles apart. At a 25th anniversary commemoration on Saturday, at least eight more victims will finally be laid to rest at the cemetery.

A quarter of a century after the events, however, the truth about what happened at Srebrenica is being subjected to a growing chorus of denial, starting in Bosnia itself and echoing around the world, moving from the fringes of the far right into mainstream discourse.

In Srebrenica, the denial starts with the mayor. The current population of around 7,000 is one-fifth of the pre-war total, and there are now more Serbs than Bosniaks, a reversal of the situation before the war and genocide. Four years ago, Srebrenica elected its first Serb mayor, Mladen Grujičić, and official rhetoric changed overnight.

Grujičić, 38, an energetic former chemistry teacher, has no time for talk of genocide. 'No Serb would deny that Bosniaks were killed here in horrible crimes... but a genocide means the deliberate destruction of a people. There was no deliberate attempt to do that here,' he said in an interview at his office in the centre of Srebrenica.

He was 10 when the war started. His father was killed during the war in a village not far from Srebrenica. Grujičić pointed out that there were victims on all sides during the conflict, which tore apart multi-ethnic Bosnia after the collapse of Yugoslavia.

But what about the international courts that have forensically sifted the evidence and come to the conclusion that the systematic slaughter around Srebrenica in July 1995 did constitute genocide, unlike other crimes during the war? 'Unfortunately, all these courts have been biased against the Serbs and this has only deepened divisions here,' he shrugged. He has not once during his time in office visited the genocide memorial, which is a five-minute drive from the town hall.

His views are in line with those of most Serb politicians in Republika Srpska, the Serb-dominated entity that makes up half of Bosnia's complicated post-war political system. Milorad Dodik, the Serb member of Bosnia's tripartite presidency, has called the Srebrenica genocide 'a fabricated myth', and the Republika Srpska authorities have set up a commission to investigate the events. Its report, due later this year, is expected to whitewash the crimes of Bosnian Serb forces.

'This is the next phase, even worse than genocide denial: to try to create a new historical reality,' said Serge Brammertz, who spent nearly a decade as chief

prosecutor at the UN international criminal tribunal for the former Yugoslavia in The Hague. The tribunal convicted the Bosnian Serb political leader Radovan Karadžić and the military commander Ratko Mladić of genocide, war crimes and crimes against humanity.

The genocide has long been an inspiration for far-right extremists and Islamophobes. The Christchurch mosque attacker last year played a song glorifying Karadžić just prior to the assault, and years earlier Anders Breivik also sought inspiration in the Balkan wars and Serb ultra-nationalism.

Recently, however, questioning the genocide has been gaining more mainstream approval. Most infuriating for survivors was the award of last year's Nobel prize for literature to the Austrian writer Peter Handke. He had delivered a eulogy at the funeral of the Serbian leader Slobodan Milošević and made a number of revisionist statements about the events of the Bosnian war that have led to accusations of genocide denial.

In a press conference before the prize-giving ceremony, when Handke was asked whether he accepted that the Srebrenica massacre had happened, he dodged the question, calling it 'empty and ignorant' and comparing it to hate mail he said he had received containing soiled toilet paper.

Emir Suljagić, who runs the sombre genocide memorial centre at Potočari, just outside Srebrenica, said: 'I am not a fan of cancel culture but if there's one thing that should cancel you, surely it's genocide denial, it's speaking at Milošević's funeral.'

The memorial centre is located in the former headquarters of the Dutch UN battalion that in July 1995 failed to protect the people gathered in

Srebrenica, which had been declared a UN safe zone. Suljagić, who survived because he worked as a translator for the mission, spoke of the trauma for returnees who have to live in places where the crimes took place. He told a story from his years working as a journalist, covering war crimes trials in The Hague.

Suljagić was watching two former Bosnian Serb soldiers give evidence against their commander at one trial. The men testified under pseudonyms and with their voice and appearance altered, but as they recounted their role in a massacre, Suljagić pieced together their identities from information given to the court. He had been to school with both of them. He assumed they had been given immunity for their role in the massacre in exchange for testifying against their commander.

'Nine years later, I'm in the parking lot of the local supermarket and one of those guys comes out and recognises me and says: 'Hi, how are you doing?' They both live locally. And I'm thinking: 'Do I tell him? Do I tell him I know?' In the end, I said nothing, but I still see them occasionally.'

With survivors and perpetrators living side by side, and given the country's divided politics, it is hard to imagine closure and reconciliation coming soon. Hasan Hasanović, who lost his twin brother and his father in the genocide, said it would be impossible to talk about progress when school trips of Serb pupils come to tour the genocide memorial, where he works as a guide.

Schooling, like so much in Bosnia, is still divided along ethnic lines. Pupils are split into separate classes for 'national subjects' such as history, and while the Bosniak textbooks cover the genocide, the

> *Serb textbooks gloss it over. There is little hope of a unified curriculum in the country in the foreseeable future. 'The main nationalist parties that continue to benefit from social division have no interest in changing a divisive status quo,' said Valery Perry, of the Democratization Policy Council in Sarajevo.*
>
> *At Srebrenica's elementary school, teachers avoid discussing the war at all, said the headmaster, Dragi Jovanović. 'Even adults, when we sit together, we simply do not touch these topics... We are trying not to hurt people's feelings, and at this point you can't educate the children without hurting their feelings,' he said.*

In June 2021, Mladić lost his appeal at ICTY against his 2017 conviction on charges of genocide. According to the New York Times, 'Confirmation of the verdict closes a grim chapter in European history.' But does it? In the wake of the confirmation of this infamous war criminal's final judgment, the ruling still leaves us with much to discover about truth, guilt and the elusive meaning of genocide. This is because the search for truth involves more than just confirming the facts.

People turn to courts in the hope and expectation that they will discover 'the truth, the whole truth, and nothing but the truth' and, in cases where crimes against humanity are being brought, tell the story of the violence that people suffered and bring perpetrators to account. In many respects, the courts *do* tell that story and o succeed in holding individuals to account. Thanks to the army of researchers at ICTY, we know more about the scope, scale, and details of atrocities that were committed in the Bosnian conflict than in nearly any other conflict in history. And because the research was carried out in the context of criminal prosecution, we know a great deal about those individuals who were directly and indirectly responsible.

But, as Eric Gordy, Professor of Political and Cultural Sociology at University College London, points outs, 'There are also some things that we do not know, and that the archives cannot not tell us. We do not understand well enough the broad set of conditions that make violence possible and we do not fully understand what violence means for those that suffer it.'

It takes more than a collection of facts to answer specific questions about the guilt or innocence of those in the dock to fulfill these demands for understanding. First is the lingering question of whether the wars in former-Yugoslavia were 'civil wars' or cross-border conflicts? Judicial findings have been vague on this aspect.

The second, and, in my view, more important, historical question that the court left unresolved is related: Did the incidents for which people were convicted comprise part of an overall plan? This is the source of the widespread frustration with the judges' repeated finding that genocide was committed in Srebrenica but nowhere else. According to Eric Gordy, it makes no sense to maintain that genocide can take place in the absence of coherent, planned and centralised authority; to create homogeneous territories by forcibly altering the demography of a population without some overarching political ambition. It is entirely possible that the answer to this question involves interpretations that may not constitute proof 'beyond all reasonable doubt' under the standards of criminal law, but that nevertheless demonstrate an intention and a pattern that are persuasive enough on their own terms to convict.

In both cases, convictions handed down by ICTY demonstrate that the wounds and tensions from a part of the world recovering from systematic large-scale violence over a quarter of a century ago cannot be addressed through processes that rely solely on the law, he suggests.

Crimes that judges are unwilling to define as 'genocide' are often referred to instead as 'crimes against humanity', themselves by no means minor offences. Before the Genocide Convention came into force in 1951, there was no higher crime under international law. Regardless, genocide is ranked as a graver crime, with the unintended consequence that prosecutors are inclined to pursue it and states are inclined—depending on whether their political leadership declares an affinity with the perpetrators or the victims—to avoid it. This is where the jobs of the lawyers and the judges become complicated.

In order to persuade a court to find that genocide has been committed, the following poorly defined elements, delineated in Article 2 of the Genocide Convention, have to be proven: First, that the acts were committed with 'an intent to destroy, in whole or in part'—both 'intent' and 'destroy' are undefined, and there is endless debate as to how big a 'part' must be—and second, that the object is a 'national, ethnical, racial or religious group'... in other words, a symbolic rather than a political or military target. Most of these contentions are difficult, if not impossible, to prove, which explains why courts around the world have made so few findings that genocide has occurred. To the degree that there is a legal debate about the rigidity of the criteria, it takes place mostly by dissent. It is possible that legal standards might change in the future so that courts are more receptive to charges of genocide, but for the foreseeable future they are not. This means that we should not expect many convictions for genocide in places like China or Myanmar anytime soon.

Meanwhile, those left behind have to grapple with their guilt. In law, the principle of 'guilt' means that people directly responsible for committing or ordering crimes would be prosecuted and the guilt would rest with them. This is, after all, a rational answer to the prevalent rhetoric of the time in which 'the Serbs' did one terrible thing, 'the Croats' another, and so on. Yet individual members of abstractly conceived groups do not—indeed, cannot—be involved, either directly or indirectly. If atrocities were committed in their name, they argue, then they were carried out without their consent by people they did not know and over whom they had no control. Identifying those individuals who actually carried out the crimes is a very convenient way of relieving whole societies of a burden they feel they do not deserve.

At the same time, there is a fundamental structural illogic to the neat legal logic. An individual can plan, order, participate in, or approve of a large-scale crime. But an individual cannot commit such a crime. The force, organisation, and equipment necessary to carry out, for example, the systematic execution of thousands of people, or the forced expulsion of tens of thousands more, are only available to institutions and states. And the will to commit a crime of this scale can only be the result of national policy, either declared or undeclared.

In the absence of any offence of 'ethnic cleansing', legal institutions are poorly equipped to deal with this set of realities. From the legalistic point of view, this may be a good thing. But from the 'never again' point of view, it makes no sense for the universe of responsibility to be restricted to a binary choice between genocide or crimes against humanity.

Unable to fit between these binary choices, the story of ethnic cleansing remains just that, a story. A story, as I said at the beginning, about the cost of lies. If everyone accepts, not just the human and moral cost but the lie itself, then the lie passes into history unchallenged to become the truth. And, as Orwell outlined so clearly when writing his seminal work 1984, 'Who controls the past, controls the future: Who controls the present controls the past.' This is how such evil becomes so constant.

www.ingramcontent.com/pod-product-compliance
Ingram Content Group UK Ltd.
Pitfield, Milton Keynes, MK11 3LW, UK
UKHW020417250726
13967UKWH00007B/2681

9 781838 490140